# Milton
## and the Middle Ages

# Milton
# and the Middle
# Ages

*Edited by* John Mulryan

*Lewisburg*
*Bucknell University Press*
*London and Toronto: Associated University Presses*

© 1982 by Associated University Presses, Inc.

Associated University Presses, Inc.
4 Cornwell Drive
East Brunswick, N.J. 08816

Associated University Presses Ltd
27 Chancery Lane
London WC2A 1NF, England

Associated University Presses
Toronto M5E 1A7, Canada

*191487*

**Library of Congress Cataloging in Publication Data**
Main entry under title:

Milton and the Middle Ages.

Includes bibliographical references.
Contents: Introduction—Angelic tact / Jason P.
Rosenblatt—Milton on the Eucharist / John C. Ulreich,
Jr.—[etc.]
1. Milton, John, 1608–1674—Knowledge and learning—
Addresses, essays, lectures.  2. Middle Ages in litera-
ture—Addresses, essays, lectures.  3. Civilization,
Medieval—Addresses, essays, lectures.  I. Mulryan,
John, 1939–
PR3592.M53M5            821'.4            81-69400
ISBN 0-8387-5036-2                        AACR2

*Printed in the United States of America*

*To my father and mother*

# Contents

# Acknowledgments

ALL of the essays in this collection were originally presented as lectures at the Kalamazoo Medieval Conference at Western Michigan University. The final versions of the essays have benefited from the comments and discussions that followed those meetings, which took place in May 1977, 1978, 1979, and 1981. In addition I wish to acknowledge permission from *Studies in Iconography* to reprint Professor Reichardt's article, "Milton's Samson and the Iconography of Wordly Vice," which originally appeared there in 1979, and permission from both Professor Labriola and the University Presses of Florida to publish the expanded version of his shorter essay, "*Christus Patiens:* The Virtue Patience and *Paradise Lost,* I-II," which originally appeared in *The Triumph of Patience: Medieval and Renaissance Studies,* ed. Gerald J. Schiffhorst, and appears here as "The Medieval View of Christian History in *Paradise Lost.*" Finally, the Bobbs-Merrill Educational Publishing Company has kindly granted me permission to reprint quotations from Milton's poetry taken from their text, *John Milton: Complete Poems and Major Prose,* ed. Merritt Y. Hughes.

# Introduction

THE title of this collection of essays, *Milton and the Middle Ages,* may seem anomalous to some. What possible sympathy could the arch-Puritan reformer, the enemy of schoolmen and episcopacy, of all manner of hierarchy and priesthood, of censorship and papal power, have with the Middle Ages? This roll call of anti-medieval epithets applied to Milton may suggest that scholars are so learned in this corner of Milton's imagination that they have forgotten an obvious truth about Milton, that he was intimately acquainted with almost all of the learning available during his time, including the classical, the medieval, and the modern.

In deference to Milton's awesome grasp of the best that was known and thought in his age, without regard to specialty, this collection takes an interdisciplinary approach to Milton and the Middle Ages, with essays on Milton's relationship to medieval theology, philosophy, history, art, and literature. The purpose of this collection is to encourage the interdisciplinary approach to Milton, and to create a more sophisticated awareness of Milton's knowledge and use of the medieval tradition. The essays complement each other in their treatment of a common theme, but they differ in their approaches and in their interpretations of Milton's use of his medieval forebears.

Jason P. Rosenblatt notes the heavily rabbinic emphasis of Raphael's commentary on creation in the seventh book of *Paradise Lost,* and its contrast to the New Testament, Christian emphasis of the blind narrator of the poem. Raphael synthesizes all of the various commentaries on Genesis known to Milton, and his speech, apropos of this collection, is rich in medieval lore. He also observes that the interest in the hexameral (six days of creation) literature of the period has caused critics to neglect medieval sources of the poem, particularly medieval rabbinic sources. At one point he suggests that Raphael's commentary may have more of a Hebraic than a Christian cast, a controversial but finely argued position that might be profitably applied to other sections of Milton's text.

John C. Ulreich attempts to reconcile the apparently anti-sacramental stance of Milton in most of his work, with those salient passages where Milton is decidedly in favor of the sacramental and even of the Eucharistic tradition. Where Rosenblatt has called our attention to Milton's use of Hebrew sources, Ulreich stresses Milton's familiarity with the theological doctrines of the medieval church, and his uneasy position as a Protestant with some affinity with and belief in Catholic doctrine. He also relates Milton's sacramentalism to medieval typology, and the figurative interpretation of sacraments in the Protestant tradition. Milton, according to Ulreich, denies the self-efficacy of the sacraments in general and of the Eucharist in particular, but he affirms the Catholic idea of participation and sees the true sacrament as residing in the human imagination, which becomes identified with the sacrament through participation in Christ.

Turning to Milton and medieval philosophy, Paul M. Dowling challenges the assumption that Milton was a pure Aristotelian and points up Milton's intellectual affinity with the medieval Catholic philosopher Thomas Aquinas (also noted by Ulreich, but in a theological context). Aquinas, like Milton, demands equal precision in discussing the moral and the intellectual virtues, while Aristotle denies the possibility of making clear distinctions among the moral virtues. Like Aquinas, Milton places faith over reason, and moves away from Aristotle and toward Aquinas in his deemphasis on habit and his identification of the art of reasoning and the art of choosing. Despite Milton's anti-scholastic bias, therefore, the famous prose tracts, *Areopagitica* and *Of Education,* are seen to be informed by medieval rather than classical philosophical principles.

Helen Goodman continues the dialogue on Milton and Aquinas, but shifts the focus of the argument from Milton's prose to his poetry. She suggests that Milton may have incorporated Aquinas's philosophical views of paradise in his poetic portrayal of Eden in *Paradise Lost.* She provides a useful summary of Aquinas's position, and indicates how Milton adapted Aquinas's view of natural causation to the Protestant view of paradise as an "unfallen world," rather than as a haven from the world's evils. Like Dowling, she takes as her point of departure Milton's remark that Spenser was "a better teacher than Scotus or Aquinas," which has unfortunately been read by most critics as a curt dismissal of the angelic doctor and all of his works.

Milton's use of the materials of history is the subject of three essays in the collection. William Melczer, in assessing the humanistic framework of Milton's tract *Of Education,* discovers a strong medieval center to the document (see also Dowling) that in some ways moves against the trend of Renaissance, particularly Italian Renaissance, humanism. Milton's interest in a pragmatic view of language and the applied arts, in a revived Aristotelianism, in universals, in spirituality and instrumentality, and in theological questions—all these interests suggest strong medieval roots for his view of education and pose a challenge to the complacent assumption that Milton was simply the last in a long line of distinguished Renaissance humanists writing on education. Even the terms *Renaissance* and *medieval* come under attack here, and we are made to realize that Milton, by virtue of his historical position in the late seventeenth century, is reacting against a different kind of tradition from that inherited by Petrarch or by any of the other distinguished continental humanists of his immediate past.

Michael Lieb places Milton in the tradition of anti-monastical satire, and indicates how Milton's distaste and contempt for monks informed all of his works, particularly *The History of Britain*. Milton, according to Lieb, blamed not only the Norman conquest on monkish corruption, but also the destruction of the married state. The monks' insistence on celibacy undermined the personal stability of marriage, and denied the possibility of divorce. Thus the historical phenomenon of anti-monastical satire and the basically medieval tradition of monasticism drew a harshly negative response from Milton, but also clearly penetrated his thought and informed his writings. In fact, at one point in his career Milton entertained the thought of writing an epic on the subject of monastical corruption, and he did provide the monks with their own mock paradise in the Paradise of Fools section in *Paradise Lost*.

· Albert Labriola combines a discussion of medieval iconography with a treatment of Milton's sense of biblical history, as interpreted through medieval sources like the *Biblia Pauperum*. Basically, Milton is using icons from the medieval tradition to discuss sacred history, for example, the iconography of the *orans*, or praying figure, who appears in the descriptions of Noah, the devil, and Christ. The image of the Leviathan is also connected by Labriola with the theme of "uncreation" and chaos in the underworld of *Paradise Lost*, a demonic parody of the creation and order in the celestial paradise above.

Paul Reichardt, in an essay devoted exclusively to iconography, explores the persistence of traditional icons and emblems of the vice or *senex*, the lustful man, and the carnal woman in medieval and Renaissance iconography, and their application to Milton's Greek-inspired drama, *Samson*

*Agonistes.* Manoa represents the wordly vice or *senex,* Dalilah love or carnality, and Haraphra the icon of huge or defiant pride. Reichardt notes Milton's use of Spenser as an iconographical source, and Milton's tendency to dramatize and particularize the more abstract icons of the earlier poet.

Roland Frye (in his *Milton's Imagery and the Visual Arts: Iconographic Tradition in the Epic Poems* (Princeton, N.J.: Princeton University Press, 1978) has recently begun the exploration of the pictorial aspects of Milton's imagination, for this is an element of Milton's genius that has not received the attention it deserves in Milton scholarship. Since Milton worked almost exclusively with biblical themes, which have yielded a rich iconographic tradition over the centuries, this will certainly prove to be a fruitful area of scholarly investigation in medieval and Milton studies in the succeeding decades.

Edward Sichi, in comparing *Paradise Lost* with the great literary masterpiece of the Middle Ages, the *Roman de la Rose,* argues persuasively that the two works share the common theme of love. He explores the many parallel images, themes, and scenes in *Paradise Lost* and the *Roman,* particularly their common philosophical approach to romantic love as an emotion that is basically deceptive and irrational. Milton, Sichi insists, knew the *Roman,* adapted many of its ideas, and profited immensely from its imagery and its structure. While there has been much distinguished work on Milton and the English medieval poets (see, for example, the fine study by A. Kent Hieatt, *Chaucer, Spenser, Milton: Mythopoeic Continuities and Transformations* [Montreal: McGill–Queens University Press, 1975]), Sichi is breaking new ground in studying Milton's relationship to a great continental work in medieval literature.

Thus the essays collected here provide a wide spectrum of views on Milton and the Middle Ages, and it is hoped that the collection will encourage scholars to study Milton, not as a medieval writer, but as a thinker and as a poet who was profoundly aware of the rich heritage of the medieval tradition, and who was perfectly capable of picking and choosing from its history, philosophy, theology, art, and literature, without necessarily accepting its version of Christianity or civil government.

JOHN MULRYAN

# Milton
# and the Middle Ages

PART I

*The Theological Dimension*

# Angelic Tact: Raphael on Creation
## Jason P. Rosenblatt

RAPHAEL'S account of creation in Book 7 of *Paradise Lost* owes much more to patristic, medieval rabbinic, and Reformation commentaries on Genesis than it does to hexameral poetry. Genesis is used to organize the bombastic verse of Sylvester's *Du Bartas* only to the extent that it keeps it from swelling indefinitely. In *Paradise Lost,* however, Raphael is in the fullest sense of the epithet a "Divine Interpreter," who joins a careful rendition of the divine word in Genesis 1 and 2 with an interlinear interpretation of that word. Raphael's dual office here is that of Mosaic voice and commentary on that voice. The direct paraphrases of Scripture in Book 7 are usually even more concise than their principal source, the King James Bible, and the interlinear poetic commentary points to a rich context of controversy. This context clarifies Milton's positions on a variety of questions. In this short essay I should like to look at Raphael's exposition in Book 7 of two angelic celebrations and one act of creation: the angelic hymns celebrating the creation of the *Ur-Licht* on the first day and the Sabbath on the seventh, and the creation of the sun on the fourth day.

After looking at these essentially extra-poetic questions in the light of exegetical tradition, I should like to note some of the ways in which Book 7 identifies itself as poetry rather than as versified treatise. In treating creation, Milton, unlike Luther and Calvin, forbears emphasizing Christ's re-creation. He resists strategies that would diminish the physical, present creation by signaling the ultimate inconsequentiality of its loss. Though faith in Christ's redemption of mankind compensates for the Fall, it also weakens the attraction of an earthly paradise. The result, in Book 7, of the poet's forbearance is the celebration of a visible, palpable universe—a celebration that is, in comparison with Christian commentaries on Genesis, purer in its sense of longing.

The first selection from Book 7, the hymn of the angels upon beholding the *Ur-Licht* of the first day, is, as we shall see, polemical evidence in determining when the angels were created. According to St. Augustine, the creation of the angels on the first day is indicated by the term *light* in the command "Let there be light."[1] Rashi, the eleventh-century rabbinical exegete, infers the creation of the angels after the first day from Genesis 1:5 (lit., "and it was evening, and it was morning, one day"): "Why is it written 'one' [rather than "the first"]? Because the Holy One, blessed be He, was alone in the universe, the angels not having been created until the second day."[2] Luther also believes that the angels were created on the second day, and treats as an "invention" the "account of a very great battle," presumably before creation, in which "the good angels withstood the evil ones."[3]

Andrew Willet, in his *Hexapla in Genesin*, surveys various opinions in considering "Why Moses omitteth the creation of the angels." He rejects Basil and Damascene, who claim "that the angels were created long before the visible world," as well as Gennadius and Achacius, who "thinke the Angels to have been created the same day with man."[4] Willet fears the earlier date, "least the Angels beeing made before the sixe daies work beganne, should be thought to have ministered unto God in the creation." Willet concludes: "to mee it seemeth more probable, that they were created upon the fourth day, when the starres and other ornaments of heaven were made."[5]

Raphael's poetic elaboration of Genesis 1:4–5, while

avoiding reference to the controversy, is nonetheless pointed. Here are the verses and their commentary:

> God saw the Light was good;
> And light from darkness by the Hemisphere
> Divided: Light the Day, and Darkness Night
> He nam'd. Thus was the first Day Ev'n and Morn:
> Nor pass'd uncelebrated, nor unsung
> By the Celestial Choirs, when Orient Light
> Exhaling first from Darkness they beheld;
> Birth-day of Heav'n and Earth; with joy and shout
> The hollow Universal Orb they fill'd,
> And touch'd thir Golden Harps, and hymning prais'd
> God and his works, Creator him they sung,
> Both when first Ev'ning was, and when first Morn.
>                                         (7.249–60)[6]

The poetic commentary begins by registering disagreement through litotes: "Nor pass'd uncelebrated nor unsung." The angels' song is ipso facto proof of their existence at this point. That they behold "Orient Light / Exhaling first from Darkness" proves that they were created before heaven and earth and before the primal light. The consistency of this view with Milton's theology is substantiated by the chapter treating creation in *Christian Doctrine.* There Milton disagrees with "most people," who understand the angels to have been created on the first day:" But that they were created on the first or any one of the six days is asserted by the general mob of theologians with, as usual, quite unjustifiable confidence. . . . The fact that they *shouted for joy* before God at the creation, as we read in Job 38:7, proves that they were then already created, not that they were first created at that time."[7] The angel Raphael, of course, buttresses his opinion on angelic creation by including the verse from Job in his commentary: the angels who fill the universe with "joy and shout" (256) are Job's sons of God who "shouted for joy."

A less demonstrable example of Milton's disagreement with received opinion, similarly registered by an initial use of understatement, can be found in the second angelic hymn in Book 7. Raphael elaborates on Genesis 2:3, a description of the first Sabbath, when God the Father,

> Now resting, bless'd and hallow'd the Sev'nth day,
> As resting on that day from all his work,
> But not in silence holy kept; the Harp
> Had work and rested not, the solemn Pipe,
> And Dulcimer, all Organs of sweet stop,
> All sounds on Fret by String or Golden Wire
> Temper'd soft Tunings, intermixt with Voice
> Choral or Unison.
>
> (7.592–99)

If, as Boyd M. Berry has recently suggested, Milton was well aware of the arguments on both sides of the Sabbatarian controversy in the seventeenth century,[8] then the description here of joyful angelic music may be read as an objection to the "Judaical" aspects of Sabbath worship. Certainly in his chapter on the Sabbath in *Christian Doctrine*, Milton professes to be "amazed" that some Christians bind themselves to this "Sinaitical precept" in "the Mosaic law."[9] "But not in silence holy kept; the Harp / Had work and rested not"—this may be an implied rejection of the Jewish prohibition against playing any musical instrument on the Sabbath. Milton's angels, who sing and play in company with the music of the spheres and thereby keep the Sabbath, differ markedly from the sober Sunday worshipers in the Reformed Church, as described in Sylvester's *Du Bartas:*

> For, by th' Almightie this great Holy-day
> Was not ordain'd to daunce, and maske, and play.

. . . . . . . . . . . . . . . . . . . . . . . . . . . . . . . . . . . . . . . . . . . . . . . .

God would, that men should in a certaine place
This Day assemble as before his face,
Lending an humble and an attentive eare
To learne his great Names deere-dread loving-feare.[10]

Raphael emphasizes joy rather than fear, the heavenly choir
rather than the heavenly host. Indeed, considering his mission to provide literal exposition, Raphael's deletion of the
word *host* (Genesis 2:1) is singular. Luther, commenting on
the word, tells us that Moses "uses military terminology in
this passage and calls the stars and the luminaries of heaven
the army or host of heaven."[11]

The long angelic Sabbath hymn contains no allusion to
Christ and his resurrection. This, too, is consistent with Milton's theology. Milton rejects Sunday as the Lord's Day: "If
it [Sunday] is the day of the Lord's resurrection, why, may I
ask, is that day to be considered the Lord's Day any more
than the day of his birth or the day of his death or the day of
his ascension? Why should we consider it more important or
more solemn than the day on which the Holy Spirit was sent
to us?"[12]

The last example, a part of Raphael's elaboration on the
creation of the sun on the fourth day, offers less striking
evidence of Milton's familiarity with exegetical tradition than
do some other examples in Book 7. These other examples
include the creation of man, which betrays Milton's anti-
trinitarian position, and the synthesis of various contradic-
tory verses from the two distinct accounts of creation in
Genesis 1 and 2. The example of the sun nourishing the stars
and planets, however, is important for what it omits—
namely, an emphasis on the Christology of creation. St. Basil,
drawing upon Philippians 2:15, notes that holy men are lights
in the world, who participate in Christ, "the true Light of the
World."[13] St. Ambrose develops the comparison between

Christ and the sun in his commentary on the fourth day: "The Son made the sun, for it was fitting that the 'Sun of Justice' should make the sun of the world."[14]

In his poem "Faith," George Herbert demonstrates the Christological implications of the sun's gift of light to the lesser heavenly bodies:

> When creatures had no reall light
> Inherent in them, thou didst make the sunne
> Impute a lustre, and allow them bright;
> And in this shew, what Christ hath done.[15]

Herbert's bright sun symbolizes the imputation of Christ's righteousness to all believers. Raphael's description of the sun, however, is notably literal and scientific rather than homiletic:

> Of Light by far the greater part he [God] took,
> Transplanted from her cloudy Shrine, and plac'd
> In the Sun's Orb, made porous to receive
> And drink the liquid Light, firm to retain
> Her gather'd beams, great Palace now of Light.
> Hither as to thir Fountain other stars
> Repairing, in thir goldern Urns draw Light,
> And hence the Morning Planet gilds her horns;
> By tincture or reflection they augment
> Thir small peculiar. . . .
>
> (7.359–68)

This is one example of Raphael's deliberate reticence in Book 7, his decision not to intimate Christian redemption. In other books of *Paradise Lost,* the narrator may use prefigurative language or even verbal irony to share a secret with the reader at a character's expense. Raphael, however, celebrates the glory of man, "the Master work" (505), and so he forbears alluding to Christ's redemption, necessitated by Adam's Fall.

Patristic and Reformation exegetes generally find occasion to introduce Christ's redemption into their account of the hexameron. Though St. Basil's nine homilies on creation constitute a word-for-word commentary on Genesis 1:1–26, the significance of their delivery within the Holy Week would not have been lost on the auditory. Andrew Willet, in his commentary on Genesis, mentions the "synode holden in Palestina by Theophilus Bishop of Cesarea, wherein it was agreed, that the world was made in the Spring, and that Christ was crucified the same day that Adam was created: at which time he also transgressed, that the first Adam herein might be a type of the second."[16]

St. Ambrose, whose sermons on creation, delivered during Holy Week, freely adapt St. Basil's text, notes the springtime occurrence of creation, the miracle at the Red Sea, and Christ's redemption of mankind:

> The sons of Israel left Egypt in the season of spring and passed through the sea, being baptized in the cloud and in the sea, as the Apostle said. At that time each year the Pasch of Jesus Christ is celebrated, that is to say, the passing over from vices to virtues, from the desires of the flesh to grace and sobriety of mind, from the unleavened bread of malice and wickedness to truth and sincerity. Accordingly, the regenerated are thus addressed: "This month shall be to you the beginning of months; it is for you the first in the months of the year."[17]

It is just, concludes Ambrose, that creation took place in the time in which the re-creation would occur.[18]

Raphael's description of the gathering of the waters on the third day evokes the miracle at the Red Sea, but only through a restrained, allusive use of imagery:

Part rise in crystal Wall, or ridge direct,
For haste; such flight the great commander impress'd
On the swift floods.

(7.293–95)

Raphael draws no connection between Old and New Testament redemption. His description here differs markedly from
that of Michael, the typologizing angel, who will find reson-
ant implications of Christian redemption in his explicit account of the Exodus in Book 12.

When the Reformers consider Genesis 1:26, the creation of
man in God's image, their arguments usually lead inexorably
to the loss of that image in the Fall and to its recovery through
Christ. To emphasize past loss and future redemption is to
blunt the immediacy of creation. Calvin, in the argument to
his commentary on creation, presents the paradigm:

he [Adam] was endued with understanding and reason, that
hee differing from brute beastes, might meditate and thinke
upon the better life; and that he might go the right way
unto God, whose image he bare. After this followeth the
fall of Adam, whereby he separated himselfe from God,
whereby it came to passe that he was deprived of all perfection. Thus Moses describeth man to be voide of all good-
nesse, blinde in minde, perverse in heart, corrupte in every
parte, and under the guilte of eternall death. But straite
after he addeth the historie of the restoring, where Christ
shineth with the benefite of redemption.[19]

Luther's nostalgia for lost innocence and paradise is explicit:

when we must discuss Paradise now, after the Flood, let us
speak of it as a historical Paradise which once was and no
longer exists. We are compelled to discuss man's state of
innocence in a similar way. We can recall with a sigh that it
has been lost; we cannot recover it in this life.[20]

Raphael, like all of Milton's angels, possesses an exquisite sense of decorum. Talking to our first parents in their state of innocence, he emphasizes their unlimited capacity to achieve virtue unmediated by any force outside themselves:

> There wanted yet the Master work, the end
> Of all yet done; a Creature who not prone
> And Brute as other Creatures, but endu'd
> With Sanctity of Reason, might erect
> His Stature, and upright with Front serene
> Govern the rest, self-knowing, and from thence
> Magnanimous to correspond with Heav'n,
> But grateful to acknowledge whence his good
> Descends, thither with heart and voice and eyes
> Directed in Devotion, to adore
> And worship God Supreme who made him chief
> Of all his works.
>
> (7.505–16)

Of course the Christian reader, who knows what is to come, is likely to find Raphael's account all the more poignant for the purity of its celebration. Yet this is accomplished with utmost tact—without the italics that would constitute a wink in the reader's direction.

The mood of Raphael's commentary in Book 7 is in a sense more Hebraic than Christian. Indeed, without making extravagant claims of influence, one might suggest that in its refusal to intimate the Fall and the Passion, Raphael's commentary resembles those of the medieval rabbinical exegetes, most notably Rashi's. Raphael's exposition is literal rather than figurative; the angel celebrates external vision ("this World/Of Heav'n and Earth *conspicuous*" [VII, 62–63]) rather than inward illumination, and he underscores the glory of unmediated human potentiality.

Finally, and inevitably when one considers a poem entitled *Paradise Lost,* Raphael's account of creation is revised and complicated by the Fall, which necessitates the redemption available only through Christ's mediation. When we turn to the beginning of Book 3, a postlapsarian invocation by a blind narrator, we discover a complete reversal of Raphael's emphases. Where Raphael celebrates the creation of Light, "first of things, quintessence pure" (7.243–44), the blind narrator invokes the Son of God as "holy Light, offspring of Heav'n first-born" (3.1). Raphael celebrates a visible, material world:

> Earth now
> Seem'd like to Heav'n, a seat where Gods might dwell,
> Or *wander* with delight, and love to *haunt*
> Her sacred Shades.
> (7.328–31; italics added)

The blind narrator's haunts are immaterial, a world of words:

> Yet not the more
> Cease I to *wander* where the Muses *haunt*
> Clear Spring, or Shady Grove, or Sunny Hill,
> Smit with the love of sacred Song.
> (7.26–29; italics added)

Raphael sings the wonder of six evenings and mornings. He describes at length the vernal bloom of the third day, the "flocks / Pasturing" (7.461–62) and the "broad Herds" upspringing (7.462) on the sixth day, and at last the creation of man in God's image. The blind narrator compresses the six days' creation into three short lines and complains that it is lost to him:

> the sweet approach of Ev'n or Morn,
> Or sight of vernal bloom, or Summer's Rose,
> Or flocks, or herds, or human face divine.
> (3.42–44)

The way back to God is lost with the Fall. Now Christ is the Way, and his mediation is necessary if paradise is to be restored. Blind to the visible creation, the narrator substitutes inward vision for eyesight, figure for letter, Christ for Adam, re-creation for creation, word for world; and, in so doing, he complicates Raphael's beautiful commentary.

## Notes

1. St. Augustine, *De Genesi ad litteram libri duodecim*, ed. and trans. P. Agaësse and A. Solignac (Bruges: De Brouwer, 1972), II. viii.16; 1:169–70: "An eo modo demonstratur primo die, quo lux facta est, conditionem spiritalis et intellectualis creaturae lucis apellatione intimari—in qua natura intelligentur omnes sancti angeli atque uirtutes."

2. Rashi, *Commentary, The Pentateuch with the Targum and the Commentaries of Rashi and Ibn Ezra*, vol. 1 (Venice, 1524–25), Gen. 1:5.

3. Martin Luther, "Lectures in Genesis" [1535–36], *Luther's Works*, ed. Jaroslav Pelikan (St. Louis, Mo.: Concordia, 1958), 1:22–23.

4. Andrew Willet, *Hexapla in Genesin* (London, 1608), p. 17.

5. Ibid., p. 18.

6. *John Milton: Complete Poems and Major Prose*, ed. Merritt Y. Hughes (New York: Odyssey, 1957), p. 352. Parenthetic book and line references to Milton's poetry are to this edition.

7. *Christian Doctrine*, in *Complete Prose Works of John Milton*, gen. ed., Don M. Wolfe (New Haven, Conn.: Yale University Press, 1953– ), 6:312; hereafter cited as *YP* with volume and page number.

8. See Boyd M. Berry, *Process of Speech: Puritan Religious Writing and Paradise Lost* (Baltimore and London: The Johns Hopkins University Press, 1976), pp. 61–101.

9. *YP*, 6:711.

10. *Bartas. His Devine Weeks and Works*, trans. Joshua Sylvester (1605: facsimile reprint Gainesville, Fla.: Scholars' Facsimiles and Reprints, 1965), p. 245.

11. Luther, "Lectures in Genesis," 1:74.

12. *YP*, 6:712.

13. St. Basil, *Exegetical Homilies*, trans. Sister Agnes Clare Way, C.D.P. (Washington, D.C.: Catholic University of America Press, 1963), p. 86.

14. St. Ambrose, *Creation, Paradise, Cain & Abel*, trans. J. J. Savage (New York: Fathers of the Church, 1961), p. 127.

15. *The Works of George Herbert*, ed. F. E. Hutchinson (Oxford: Clarendon, 1941). p. 51.

16. Willet, *Hexapla in Genesin*, p. 10.

17. St. Ambrose, *Creation*, p. 13.

18. Ibid., 13.

19. John Calvin, *Commentarie upon the first books of Moses called Genesis*, trans. Thomas Tymme (London, 1578), p. 21.

20. *Luther's Works*, 1:90.

## [ 2 ]
# Milton on the Eucharist: Some Second Thoughts about Sacramentalism

*John C. Ulreich, Jr.*

SOME acrimonious and surly Miltonist, looking askance at the superscription of this essay, might be provoked to exclaim: "Bless us! Milton on the Eucharist? What a word on a title page is this?" And even one more sympathetic to remote allusions and obscure opinions might not unreasonably ask whether Milton ever had any second thoughts about the sacraments—or whether we need have any. Surely his views are plain enough, and well enough known, to discourage any "vague subtleties of speculation": "Why does our imagination shy away from a notion of God which he himself does not hesitate to promulgate in unambiguous terms?"[1] Milton himself does not shy away from promulgating his notion of the Eucharist in terms that are neither ambiguous nor accommodating:

> The papist Mass is not at all the same as the Lord's Supper . . . . the Mass brings down Christ's holy body from its supreme exaltation at the right hand of God. It drags it back to the earth, though it has suffered every pain and hardship already, to a state of humiliation even more wretched and degrading than before: to be broken once more and crushed and ground, even by the fangs of brutes. (pp. 559–60)

Besides arguing specifically—and vehemently—against the "monstrous" doctrine of transubstantiation (p. 554), Milton's criticism of the Mass suggests a radical antipathy toward sacramentalism in general—toward the idea, that is, that any merely physical action may be a vehicle of grace, or that spirit may somehow be *incarnate*, made manifest in flesh: "not teeth but faith is needed to eat his flesh" (p. 553). As more than one critic has been led to observe, and as J. B. Broadbent has forcefully argued, the tendency of Milton's thought, and of the language in which it is expressed, is "away from the incarnate towards the ideate."[2] Whereas the poetry of the Middle Ages—of Dante, or Langland, or Chaucer—or even (to a lesser extent) the poetry of Spenser, is felt to be essentially conservative, Catholic, communal, and concrete, Milton's poetry is widely perceived as revolutionary, Protestant, individual, and abstract—in a word, anti-sacramental.

Furthermore, Milton's iconoclastic assault on the sacraments seems quite consistent with his Protestant antipathy to Catholic forms of worship and belief and with his humanistic aversion to medieval modes of thought and expression. His writings offer abundant evidence of his hostility to the "sensuall Idolatry" of "outward conformity" and to the "excremental whiteness" of an "implicit faith" and of his profound contempt for the "vague subtleties" of scholastic theology.[3] Despite C. S. Lewis's claim that, in *Paradise Lost*, "the Hierarchical idea . . . is the indwelling life of the whole work," Milton's attitude toward what Lewis (and others) called "the medieval synthesis" is at best deeply ambivalent.[4] One prominent feature of that synthesis is a predilection, usually described as "sacramental," for perceiving concrete phenomena, not merely as objects of sense, but as vital embodiments of spirit. Indeed, a truly hierarchical conception of the universe presupposes such an experience of physical nature as inherently significant, so that, as Owen Barfield has observed, "phenomena themselves" possess "the sort of mul-

tiple significance which we to-day only find in symbols."[5] To
a sacramental consciousness, participating in phenomena as
representations of spirit, the whole of created nature is felt to
be the garment of God, not merely "answering" but *incarnat-
ing* "his great Idea" (*PL* 7.557).[6] Milton, however, does not
appear to have experienced phenomena in this way. His radical iconoclasm and his professed antipathy to the whole tex-
ture of medieval thought would seem to argue that Milton's
thinking is necessarily anti-sacramental: "the mere flesh is of
no use here" (p. 553). And this has been the prevailing view of
Milton's poetry: that it is, in Broadbent's phrase, "deficient in
body."[7] Despite persuasive dissent from critics like
Rosemond Tuve,[8] Malcolm Ross would appear to have
settled the sacramental question when he argued that Milton's
radical Protestantism led him to disintegrate Eucharistic symbols "in an urge to purify the idea."[9] Even William Madsen,
arguing the typological, hence medieval, basis of Milton's
symbolism concedes that Milton's mind is strongly bent
"away from the material and toward the spiritual."[10] In a
word, Milton's poetry is "ideate" or "spiritual" *rather than*
"incarnational" or "sacramental."

Nonetheless, recent scholarship has substantially modified
our view of Milton's relation to the Middle Ages by suggesting a number of affinities between his thinking and habits of
mind that are usually thought of as distinctively medieval.
William B. Hunter, Jr., and C. A. Patrides, for example,
have shown us Milton's extensive reliance upon those scholastic subtleties which he professed to despise.[11] And recent
typological and iconographic studies of Milton's symbolism
have disclosed profound analogies between Milton's poetry
and the art of the Middle Ages.[12] Most recently, in this collection, Albert Labriola has adduced abundant iconographic
evidence to demonstrate Milton's essentially medieval view of
history in *Paradise Lost*. The cumulative force of such studies
suggests that Milton is not so much uniformly antipathetic to
medieval influence as he is rigorously selective in his response

to influences of any kind. He is not a syncretist like Spenser, but neither is he an absolutist like Hobbes; in matters of tradition, as in the decorum of art, the poet's way (as opposed to the polemicist's) lies *in medias res,* between the extremes of uncritical acceptance and absolute rejection.[13] Milton adapts and transforms his medieval inheritance, sometimes radically, but he remains at the same time profoundly sympathetic to certain medieval modes of thought and expression.

In the light of such elective affinities, it seems appropriate to reexamine Milton's idea of sacramental analogy and to challenge certain conclusions that have been based on a partial reading of the evidence. Toward that end I should like to suggest that Milton's view of the sacraments is more complex than is usually supposed. At the very least, his poetic practice in *Paradise Lost* is not wholly consistent with the theory of the sacraments set forth in the *Christian Doctrine*. Milton may or may not have had second thoughts as he was composing his epic, but the idea of a sacrament presented there is certainly more complex, and less narrowly Protestant, than his uncompromising discussion in the treatise would lead one to expect. Furthermore, his view of sacramental signification has a direct bearing on his ideas about the use of figurative language and hence on his beliefs about the nature of poetic meaning. By exploring some of these imaginative implications, I hope to clarify, and perhaps reconcile, the apparent inconsistencies between Milton's iconoclastic doctrine and his iconic poetry. To the extent that such a reconciliation seems possible, it strongly suggests that Milton's iconoclasm has a sacramental basis and that we should indeed think of him as in some sense a sacramental poet.

I

Traditionally, a sacrament in general, and the Eucharist in particular, implies *communion:* the participation of believers in Christ. According to the orthodox view, represented by Aquinas, that participation is physical as well as spiritual: the material sacrament is a "sacred thing, a sign which [in and of itself] sanctifies men"; it is "the visible figure of invisible grace, bearing its likeness and *serving as its cause.*" Indeed, the sign and its significance, the matter and form of a sacrament, are inseparable: "sacramental signification is combined from sensible things and words, which are like matter and form and make a unity." To partake of Communion, therefore, is to participate *substantially* in the Christ, in body as well as soul, through an incarnation: "this sacrament, in which *Christ is really present* [through the transubstantiation of the elements], is the culmination of all the other sacraments in which his power is shared.[14]

Against this characteristically medieval idea, Milton's reductive, Protestant conception stands in sharp contrast.[15] In the first place, participation in the sacrament is wholly spiritual: "the mere flesh is of no use here" (p. 553), for "it is the Spirit which gives life and it is faith which feeds" (p. 557). Consequently, "the Papists are wrong when they attribute to the outward sign the power of conferring salvation or grace" (p. 556). Moreover, sacramental meaning does not arise from a simple unity of matter and form: the visible sacrament is merely an "external seal" of internal grace, a "representation through certain outward signs" of that which is in itself invisible (p. 542). Given this absolute separation of matter and form, there can be no question of Christ's real presence in the sacramental elements; the idea of transubstantiation is "utterly alien to reason, common sense and human behavior" (p. 554).

All of this seems perfectly straightforward—and almost doggedly anti-sacramental. The matter becomes more complex, however, when we attempt to place Milton's doctrine in the context of his work as a whole. The absolute separation of matter and spirit does not accord very well with his monism, which leads him to argue a material basis for Creation and which manifests itself so conspicuously in the metaphysical passages of *Paradise Lost*.[16] Furthermore, in certain poetic contexts Milton seems to affirm doctrines that he had explicitly denied in the *Christian Doctrine*. One of these apparent contradictions is especially pertinent to the present investigation. In the treatise Milton excoriates the doctrine of transubstantiation as tantamount to "cannibalism": "Consubstantiation and particularly transubstantiation and papal ἀνϑρωποφαγία or cannibalism" are "monstrous" doctrines (p. 554). In *Paradise Lost*, however, Milton uses the word *transubstantiate* (*PL* 5.438) to describe the process by which *corporal nutriments* (496) are converted to the *proper substance* (493) of one who consumes them. This is precisely the point denied in the *Christian Doctrine:* "if we eat his flesh it will not remain in us, but, to speak candidly, after being digested in the stomach, it will be at length exuded" (p. 554).[17] And this point, so emphatically denied in the treatise, is affirmed with equal emphasis in *Paradise Lost*. Raphael insists that he converts the material food of Paradise into his own "intelligential substance" (5.408) by a physiological process of concoction, digestion, and assimilation that transforms "corporeal to incorporeal" (413). Now, the very possibility of such a transformation presupposes that body and spirit are composed of a single substance, that matter and form are, in fact, *consubstantial*. The twenty-eighth chapter of the *Christian Doctrine* denies this community of substance. Milton rejects not only the theological doctrine of consubstantiation, but the metaphysical postulate from which the doctrine is derived: the idea that matter and form constitute a unity. He argues that the relation between fiesh and spirit is "external" (p. 543) rather than intrinsic, an "analogy" or "figure of speech" (p. 555) rather than an actual unity. Elsewhere in the treatise, however, Milton affirms the consubstantiality of matter and form. In chapter 7, form and matter, "action" and "passivity," are treated as "relative terms"—as aspects of a single divine substance (*substantia*),

out of which God made the world (pp. 306–8).[18] And this
idea of consubstantiality is triumphantly asserted in *Paradise
Lost:*

> O *Adam,* one Almighty is, from whom
> All things proceed, and up to him return
> If not deprav'd from good, created all
> Such to perfection, one first matter all,
> Indu'd with various forms, various degrees
> Of substance, and in things that live, of life.
>
> (5.469–74)

Now, the consubstantiality of matter and form is the crux
of the whole sacramental problem. The Catholic theory of the
sacraments presupposes a community of body and spirit, so
that—in Milton's words!—"man is a living being, intrinsically and properly one and individual . . . not double or separable: not, as is commonly thought, produced from and composed of two different and distinct elements, soul and body"
(*CD*1.7, p. 318). It is precisely this consubstantiality that
allows body to be transformed—or digested—into spirit.[19]
The treatise rejects the possibility of such a metamorphosis;
once digested, the physical body of Christ becomes mere
excrement. In *Paradise Lost,* however, Milton asserts the absolute transformation of corporeal into incorporeal:

> Man's nourishment, by gradual scale sublim'd
> To vital spirits aspire[s], to animal,
> To intellectual, give[s] both life and sense,
> Fancy and understanding, whence the Soul
> Reason receives, and reason is her being.
>
> (5.483–87)

In Milton's vision of innocent human nature, body and spirit
constitute an indissoluble unity, whose elements differ in degree but are of the same *kind*, so that human nature itself is

sacramental. Indeed, the whole of paradise is sacramental in the fullest possible sense of the word. As J. B. Broadbent observes, the meal that Adam and Eve share with Raphael is plainly a "sacramental occasion," and Milton's conception of Creation "implies a notion of the Church as indeed the body of God on earth, so that sacraments and symbols are actualised."[20] Milton's conception of the paradisal relation between Adam and Eve is equally sacramental. Despite his argument in the *Christian Doctrine* that "matrimony . . . should clearly not . . . be called a sacred thing at all, let alone a sacrament" (p. 561), Milton's epic voice celebrates "wedded Love" as the "mysterious Law" of human nature, "true source / Of human offspring, sole propriety / In Paradise of all things common else" (4.750–52). United in this mystery, Adam and Eve are not merely one in spirit; they are "one Flesh, one Heart, one Soul" (8.499). Whatever Milton's professed beliefs in the *Christian Doctrine*, his poetic vision of paradise is plainly sacramental.

## II

How, then, are we to reconcile the apparent contradiction between the secularizing arguments of the treatise and the sacramental vision of the epic? And how are we to account for Milton's provocative use of the word *transubstantiate* (*PL*5.438)? One way of dealing with the problem is to acknowledge—or assert—the contradiction. Broadbent argues, for example, that Milton's sacramental vision of Eden is an aberration: the "literal" and substantial "doctrine that man is created in the image of God" simply "runs to waste in the poem."[21] And Madsen's discussion of Milton's symbolism comes to essentially the same conclusion. Arguing that "the symbolism of *Paradise Lost* is typological rather than Platonic," he finds that "everything Raphael says about the symbolic correspondences between Heaven and earth, the ascent

of the soul, and the ladder of love . . . is undercut by the fact
that he is speaking of unfallen man in an unfallen world. He
represents, as it were, the highest reach of the pagan intellect."[22] But dismissing the vision of paradise as in some way
apart from Milton's usual symbolic practice does violence to
the imaginative coherence of the epic. Broadbent's misper-
ception of Milton's symbolism leads him to conclude that
*Paradise Lost* has only the kind of "obvious formal unity
conferred by heroic verse and structure, and the obvious
ideological relation between such themes as the Fall, Creation, War in Heaven, astronomy, scale of being, angelology,"
that Milton's epic lacks the more intense unity of "a Shakespeare play or a Lawrence novel," in which "dramatic and
lyrical phases . . . closely reciprocate to form an 'organic'
whole."[23] Madsen's view of the poem is more nearly organic,
but his division between Raphael's Neoplatonic symbolism
and Milton's typology seems somewhat arbitrary and over-
ingenious. Although Milton's symbolism is typological in
roughly the way that Madsen suggests, typology does not
preclude Neoplatonic structures of thought and expression:
witness their fruitful interpenetration in Spenser's poetry.[24]
Still less does typology preclude the kind of metaphoric reso-
nance that I have called "sacramental."[25] On the whole, I find
it difficult to accept the notion that Milton's vision is apparently sacramental in one place and radically secular in
another. On the contrary, the architectonic coherence of Milton's epic argues the presence of a common metaphoric substrate underlying the varieties of Neoplatonic, typological,
and other symbolic structures. Whether that substrate can
properly be called "sacramental" is, of course, another question, with which I shall deal presently.

Another way of accounting for apparent inconsistencies in
Milton's thinking is to attribute them to the different dispen-
sations of prose and poetry: whereas Milton speaks discur-

sively and literally in the treatise, the epic allows him the license of metaphoric intuition.[26] But this sharp distinction between treatise and poem seems somewhat arbitrary, inasmuch as it fails to account for the substantial agreement between the two works.[27] The ready and easy divorce of poetry from prose does not help much to resolve apparent inconsistencies within the treatise itself, and it ignores large sections of discursive exposition within the epic. Furthermore, the positivistic attempt to treat the symbolic language of *Paradise Lost* as metaphoric *rather than* literal blandly contradicts what Milton says in the treatise about the severe limitations of merely figurative language. Milton's claims for the absolute validity of his fiction are emphatic and unremitting: Hesperian fables are true in paradise (4.250–51).[28] In the spirit of accommodation, Milton employs the golden fruit, "not so much for what it really is as for what it illustrates or signifies" (p. 555), but this figurative limitation does not apply either to "the Fruit / . . . whose mortal taste / Brought Death into the World" (*PL*1.1–3) or to the "flow'rs and thir fruit" that become "Man's nourishment" (5.482–83). These fruits are literal *as well as* spiritual; they are the concrete, metaphoric embodiment of the ideas they signify.

In the *Christian Doctrine* Milton seems to insist on an absolute dichotomy of flesh and spirit, literal meaning and figurative. "Not teeth" he argues, "but faith is needed to eat . . . [Christ's] flesh" (p. 553). In *Paradise Lost*, however, he frequently denies this sharp distinction between letter and spirit. The physiological process of digestion is sometimes used figuratively to illustrate mental activity: "Knowledge is as food, and needs no less / Her Temperance over Appetite" (7.126–27). But processes that are here distinguished by simile are elsewhere united in metaphor. Consider, for example, Milton's primary analogy for the transformation of body into spirit:

                    So from the root
Springs lighter the green stalk, from thence the leaves
More aery, last the bright consummate flow'r
Spirits odorous breathes: flow'rs and thir fruit
Man's nourishment, by gradual scale sublim'd
To vital spirits aspire, to animal,
To intellectual, give both life and sense,
Fancy and understanding, whence the Soul
Reason receives, and reason is her being.

                                      (5.479–87)

In this analogy, the conjunctive adverb *So* introduces an instance rather than a simile, a concrete manifestation of the
process that has just been abstractly defined. Both plant and
man participate in the process of cosmic evolution. As a consequence, the image of the plant functions, not merely to
"illustrate or signify," but to *substantiate* the concept of organic growth, which is both material and spiritual. The
metamorphosis of the plant from root to flower and fruit is a
metaphor of spiritual transformation, not a mere figure of
speech, because the relation of image to idea is an identity
rather than a mere likeness. Material growth and spiritual
sublimation are not discrete processes; they are, rather, interdependent phases of a single process, "Differing but in
degree, of kind the same" (490). And because every higher
activity contains within itself the lower functions that it sub-
sumes (409–10), the development of the human organism recapitulates the growth of the plant. Conversely, the
metamorphosis of the plant participates in the transformation
of the human being, so that the relation of image to idea is
also a relation of part to whole. The growing plant is a symbol, in Coleridge's terms, rather than a mere similitude: it
"partakes of the reality which it renders intelligible."[29]
  The implications of this symbol are plainly sacramental,
inasmuch as the very possibility of such participation presupposes that matter and form, body and spirit, image and idea,

are consubstantial. And the sacramentalism implicit in this image is inextricably woven into the fabric of the poet's vision. The complementary biological processes of digestion and growth constitute Milton's primary metaphor for the spiritual process by which the whole of Creation, "animate with gradual life / Of Growth, Sense, Reason," is "all summ'd up in Man" (9.112–13), transformed and *transplanted* (3.293), as it were *transubstantiated* in the body of "one greater Man" (1.4).

## III

Now, if Milton's vision of the Invisible Church as the body of Christ is indeed sacramental in the way I have suggested, we may be in a position to clarify somewhat his use of the word *transubstantiate* (5.438). In the first place, we must observe that the word is used to denote a *natural* process of transformation; in context, the technical term emphasizes the materiality even of angelic substance. Saint Thomas uses the term *transubstantiate* exclusively to denote the sacramental conversion of the elements in the Mass: this conversion "is not a transmutation or transformation; it is not catalogued under the ordinary physical processes, but is given the special name of transubstantiation."[30] Milton's use of the term robs it of its special significance, in effect denying "the common gloss / Of Theologians" (5.435–36). It seems unlikely, however, that Milton chose this controversial term merely in order to jibe at the "vague subtleties" of the schoolmen. By relegating transubstantiation to one of the "ordinary physical processes," Milton does, in fact, secularize the sacred mystery of the Mass; at the same time, however, he exalts the ordinary physical process of digestion into a sacramental act: "whatever was created" is "sustain'd and fed," so that every higher degree of life and substance contains within itself "every lower faculty" (5.414, 415, 410). It would seem, there-fore, that Milton's use of *transubstantiate* is consistent with his belief that the universe was created out of some primal matter, "a substance . . . derivable from no other source than from the fountain of every substance, though at first confused and formless, being afterwards adorned and digested into or-der by the hand of God" (*CD* 1.7; *Works*, 15:23).

Furthermore, Milton's use of the technical term suggests that, although he emphatically rejects the Catholic dogma, he embraces certain of its philosophical and imaginative implica-tions—chiefly the idea of *participation*. His use of the Catho-lic term, even if faintly disparaging, emphasizes his philosophical conviction that body participates in spirit, that matter and form are *substantially* one: "one first matter all / Indu'd with various forms, various degrees / Of substance" (PL 5.472–75). The theological corollary of this idea is the belief that sacraments imply a *substantial* participation in the person of Christ; Milton consistently affirms this belief, im-plicitly in his definition of "[supernatural] REGENERA-TION" as an "INGRAFTING IN CHRIST," whereby "THE WHOLE MAN, BOTH SOUL AND BODY, IS SANCTIFIED" (*CD* 1.18, p. 461), and explicitly in his asser-tion that the sacrament of Baptism signifies our actual "UN-ION WITH CHRIST THROUGH HIS DEATH, BURIAL AND RESURRECTION" (1, 28, p. 544). So far there is broad agreement between Aquinas and Milton on the ques-tion of sacramental participation: the essence of a sacrament is *communion* with Christ.[31]

Where Catholic and Protestant part company is over the question of sacramental efficacy. For Aquinas, we recall, the physical sacrament is a *cause* of grace: because sacraments are the instruments of the Word Incarnate, it is "fitting . . . that he should come through to men in bodily fashion, and that divine virtue should continue to work invisibly in them through visible appearances."[32] This notion Milton categorically rejects: he insists that "sacraments cannot impart salvation or grace of themselves" (p. 556). And this radical difference between an efficacious sign *(signum efficax)* and a mere outward sign *(signum externum)* entails a very different conception of sacramental significance. For Aquinas, the matter and form of a sacrament, the sign and the thing signified, constitute an indissoluble unity: "Thus the washing by baptismal water represents the interior cleansing from sin which is caused in virtue of the sacrament of baptism."[33] For Milton, however, the sign is *merely* a seal or representation, a figure of speech:[34] "we are not saved by that outward baptism which washes away merely the filth of the flesh, but, as Peter says, *by the obligation of a good conscience*" (p. 545). He repeatedly emphasizes that sacramental actions are only figurative: "a thing which in any way illustrates or signifies another thing is mentioned not so much for what it really is as for what it illustrates or signifies" (p. 555).[35]

It is precisely at this point, where Milton departs most radically from Catholic tradition, that his own position begins to seem inconsistent. On the one hand, he insists that body and soul are one substance, "that man is a living being, intrinsically and properly one and individual . . . not double or separable: not, as is commonly thought, produced from and composed of two different and distinct elements, soul and body" (*CD* 1.7, p. 318). One might expect him, therefore, to affirm an analogous identity between corporal sign and spiritual significance—especially "in the sacraments, where the relation between the symbol and the thing symbolized is very close" (p. 555). Instead, he insists on an absolute separation of visible from invisible, external from internal, image from idea: "If under a fleshly covenant . . . [the Jews] ate a spiritual Christ, then certainly we, under a spiritual covenant, do not eat a fleshly Christ" (p. 554). How, then, is it possible for the poet to "relate / To human sense th' invisible exploits / of warring Spirits . . . By lik'ning spiritual to corporal forms, / As may express them best" (*PL* 5.564–66, 573–74)?[36] Milton's literal-minded assault on sacramental meaning seems to deny the possibility of valid metaphor.

## IV

The question we must ask ourselves, then, is how Milton could have been led to espouse a position that appears self-contradictory and that has the effect of cutting him off, intellectually, from the sources of his own poetic inspiration. The best way to approach this question, I believe, is to inquire more closely into the nature of sacramental *participation*.

For Aquinas, to say that we participate in a sacrament means that we experience its phenomenal elements—the bread and wine—not as mere sense data but as *representations* of spirit, the transubstantial body and blood of Christ. The meaning of the sacramental sign depends, therefore, on its being the actual expression of the thing signified, so that the physical elements themselves are felt to be charged with symbolic meaning. As Barfield has observed, not the idea of participation merely, but participation "as an actual experience," was fundamental to Aquinas's thinking, so that his perception of the Eucharist was necessarily symbolic.[37]

Milton does not experience phenomena in this way. Spirit does not manifest itself to sense perception: the soul has no need of the "weak, and fallible office of the senses."[38] Appearances are not participated in as representations of spirit: "all corporeal resemblances of inward holiness & beauty are now past."[39] So it is that the relation between a sign and its significance seems purely figurative and conventional—nominal rather than actual. A sign does not participate in its significance. A figure of speech may *imply* or *shadow* spirit but does not contain or manifest it: "not teeth but faith is needed to eat his flesh" (p. 553).[40] A verbal sign is *either* literal, as the word *teeth* is, *or* figurative, as *eat* is, but not both simultaneously. From this radical disjunction arises the profound difference between a sacramental representation and a mere "figure of speech."[41] Milton's experience of the sacrament is figurative precisely because he does not participate in the Eucharistic phenomena.

But if Milton experiences the sacrament only nominally, ought we to use the word *participate* at all in connection with that experience? I believe that we should, provided we distinguish carefully the manner in which such participation is imagined. I have observed that Milton does not conceive of phenomena as representations of spirit in external nature, but I might better have begun by asking what it is that phenomena do represent: if not the spirit acting through appearances, what then? The answer is implicit in virtually every line of Milton's epic: phenomenal nature is—or is to become—the representation of man himself: "Creatures animate with gradual life / Of Growth, Sense, Reason," are "all summ'd up in Man" (9.112–13). As figures of speech, the products of the poet's conscious imagination, images represent the power of the spirit working, not in nature, but within ourselves.

The kind of immediate participation reflected in Aquinas's thinking is largely involuntary and unreflective. Spontaneity of this kind is amply illustrated by sacramental imagery even in the most self-conscious medieval poetry. In *Pearl*, for example, shortly after his awakening the Dreamer rediscovers the substance of his vision in his everyday experience: "Krystes dere blessyng and myn / . . . in the forme of bred and wyn."[42] As Paul Piehler has observed, "the eucharistic transformation of the earthly symbol to the heavenly reality . . . confirms the participatory parallelism between Christ's death and resurrection on the one hand and the dreamer's deadly sleep and reawakening on the other."[43] From the Dreamer's point of view, this participation is largely unconscious; it is part of his immediate experience of life rather than a conclusion deductively arrived at or a course of action deliberately chosen.

For Milton, on the other hand, participation in a sacrament always requires a conscious act of will: "that living bread which, Christ says, is his flesh, and the true drink which, he says, is his blood, can only be the doctrine which teaches us that Christ was made man in order to pour out his blood for us. The man who accepts this doctrine with true faith will live for ever" (p. 553). For faith of this explicit kind "both understanding and will are requisite" (p. 547); the communion that results is grounded in our *conscious* "participation through the spirit."[44] And what we are conscious of, primarily, is not the activity of nature without us but the working of our own minds. The sacrament is "a kind of symbol" of that inner activity (p. 552). The reality in which such symbols participate, and which they render intelligible, is the spirit within man himself. Appearances do not contain spirit; rather, they are contained by it: "spirit, being the more excellent substance, virtually, as they say, and eminently contains within itself what is clearly the inferior substance; in the same way as the spiritual and rational faculty contains the corporeal, that is, the sentient and vegetative faculty" (*CD* 1.7, p. 309). Our communion with Christ in the sacraments depends upon the activity of this spiritual and rational faculty, upon the operation of mind and will. It is in this sense, I believe, that it is appropriate to speak of Milton's participating in the sacrament, by a conscious act of imagination.

## V

In *Saving the Appearances*, Owen Barfield has explored the differences between *original participation*, in which spirit is experienced, mythically, outside of man, and what he calls *final participation,* in which, by becoming conscious of our own imaginative activity, we experience the spirit within ourselves. "Original participation fires the heart from a source outside itself; the images enliven the heart. But in final participation—since the death and resurrection—the heart is fired from within by the Christ; and it is for the heart to enliven the images."[45] The Eucharist was—or ought to have been—the primary means by which the transformation from original to final participation was accomplished:

> All who partake of the Eucharist first acknowledge that the man who was born in Bethlehem was "of one substance with the Father by whom all things were made"; and then they take that substance into themselves, together with its representations named bread and wine. . . . There was no difficulty in understanding it, as long as enough of the old participating consciousness survived. It was only as this faded, it was only as a "substance" behind the appearances grdually ceased to be an experience and dimmed to a hypothesis or a credo, that the difficulties and doctrinal disputes concerning transubstantiation began to grow. (P. 170)

Milton does not experience the sacramental elements as representations of the divine substance, and so he rejects the doctrine of transubstantiation. He does, however, recognize the existence of that spiritual substance within himself, so that sacramental images become the expression of his own imaginative energy. As Madsen has argued, Milton "creates his own types."[46] When he proclaims that "all corporeal resemblances . . . are *now* past," his use of the adverb suggests his awareness of a time when matter did manifest spirit, when men participated in the phenomena themselves as representations of an indwelling spirit. Now, however, that spirit dwells only within ourselves. Milton's prophetic iconoclasm, like his rejection of transubstantiation, expresses his

awareness that original participation—"the old-cast vestments . . . of sensuall Idolatry"[47]—must be destroyed "precisely in order that it might be reborn"[48] as "a paradise
within" (*PL* 12.587). The apparent inconsistency in Milton's
treatment of body and spirit is to be accounted for by this
tension between original and final participation, between
meaning given as inspiration and meaning made by imagination. When he speaks of likening spiritual to corporeal forms
as though they could be identified, or when he speaks of
matter and form as one substance, of potency digested into
act,[49] Milton harks back to the older, inspirational mode of
participation. But when he speaks of spirit containing body,
as the more excellent substance, "all summ'd up in Man," he
looks forward to the imaginative mode of final participation,
the paradise within.

Milton has, in effect, transformed the sacrament from an
unconscious instrument of grace into a conscious metaphor of
spirit. That metaphor derives, not from the usage of medieval
scholasticism, but from Augustine's definition of sacramental
significance as "the mystery [*sacramentum*] of the Old Testament, in which the New was hidden."[50] The physical sacrament is a *type* of the spiritual significance hidden within it, a
*shadow* of truth that has been accommodated to man's limited
understanding,[51] and a foreshadowing of truth that is to be
more fully revealed. As man grows spiritually, "by gradual
scale sublim'd" (*PL* 5.483), his understanding is enlarged and
clarified, typologically, so that he progresses

> From shadowy Types to Truth, from Flesh to Spirit,
> From imposition of strict Laws, to free
> Acceptance of large Grace, from servile fear
> To filial, works of Law to works of Faith.
>
> (12.303–6)

The basis of this typological growth is an organic transformation from material substance to spiritual, from the

moribund appearance of things outside of us to the living reality within, from inspiration by the Word to a fully realized imagination of the Word. And as man is transformed in the Christ, so that God becomes "All in All" (3.341), the human imagination itself becomes "the radiant image of his Glory" (3.63), "substantially express'd" (3.140). In final participation, the human imagination, working to actualize the Christ, becomes the sacrament.

## Notes

1. *Christian Doctrine* 1.2, trans. John Carey, in *Complete Prose Works of John Milton*, ed. Maurice Kelley (New Haven, Conn.: Yale University Press, 1973), 6: 134, 136. Milton's discussion of the sacraments is found in chap. 28, "Of the External Sealing of the Covenant of Grace" *(De obsignatione foederis gratiae externa)*. Unless otherwise noted, I quote throughout from Carey's translation in *Complete Prose Works*, hereafter cited as *CPW* 6 or referred to simply by page number. In cases where the meaning of Milton's Latin might be in question I have referred to James Holly Hanford's edition of the text and to Bishop Charles R. Sumner's translation in *The Works of John Milton*, ed. Frank Allen Patterson et al. (New York: Columbia University Press, 1934), vols. 14–17, hereafter cited as *Works*.

2. J. B. Broadbent, "The Nativity Ode," in *The Living Milton: Essays by Various Hands*, ed. Frank Kermode (New York: Macmillan, 1960), p. 23.

3. *Apud Of Reformation Touching Church-Discipline in England, Areopagitica, Christian Doctrine* 1.2 (*CPW*, 1: 520, 522; 2: 516; 6: 134).

4. C. S. Lewis, *A Preface to Paradise Lost* (London: Oxford University Press, 1942), p. 79, and *The Discarded Image: An Introduction to Medieval and Renaissance Literature* (Cambridge: Cambridge University Press, 1964), p. 11. In the latter work Lewis explores in persuasive detail "the whole organization of . . . [medieval] theology, science, and history into a single, complex, harmonious mental Model of the Universe" (p. 11), but the precise applicability of that model to Milton's universe remains moot.

5. Owen Barfield, *Saving the Appearances: A Study in Idolatry* (London: Faber and Faber, 1957), p. 74. He observes that "the essence of symbolism is, not that words or names, as such, but that things or events themselves, are apprehended as representations" of that which does not itself appear to the senses.

6. Milton's poetry is quoted from *John Milton: Complete Poems and Major Prose*, ed. Merritt Y. Hughes (New York: Odyssey Press, 1957).

7. Broadbent, "The Nativity Ode," p. 17.

8. Rosemond Tuve, *Images and Themes in Five Poems by Milton* (Cambridge, Mass.: Harvard University Press, 1962), p. 5, argues that "Milton's figurative habits melt indistinguishably into those of the modified medieval background against which we see him."

9. Malcolm MacKenzie Ross, *Poetry and Dogma: The Transfiguration of*

*Eucharistic Symbols in Seventeenth-Century English Poetry* (New Brunswick, N.J.: Rutgers University Press, 1954), p. 157.

10. William Madsen, *From Shadowy Types to Truth: Studies in Milton's Symbolism* (New Haven, Conn.: Yale Universty Press, 1968), p. 70. Although the question of Milton's sacramentalism is now seldom explicitly raised, it is almost always implicitly denied. Stanley Fish's idiosyncratic reading of Milton, for example, presupposes that the basis of Milton's poetry is individual *rather than* communal, spiritual *rather than* incarnational or sacramental.

11. See, especially, C. A. Patrides, *Milton and the Christian Tradition* (Oxford: Clarendon Press, 1966), and William B. Hunter, Jr., C. A. Patrides, and J. H. Adamson, *Bright Essence: Studies in Milton's Theology* (Salt Lake City: University of Utah Press, 1971).

12. See, for example, Jason P. Rosenblatt, "The Mosaic Voice in *Paradise Lost*," and Albert C. Labriola, "The Aesthetics of Self-Diminution: Christian Iconography and *Paradise Lost*," both in *Milton Studies*, ed. Albert C. Labriola and Michael Lieb, vol. 7 (Pittsburgh, Pa.: University of Pittsburgh Press, 1975). My essay on "The Typological Structure of Milton's Imagery," *Milton Studies*, vol. 5 (Pittsburgh, Pa.: University of Pittsburgh Press, 1970), touches on some of Milton's relations to medieval allegory. Barbara Kiefer Lewalski, "Typological Symbolism and the 'Progress of the Soul' in Seventeenth-Century Literature," in *Literary Uses of Typology: from the Late Middle Ages to the Present* (Princeton, N.J.: Princeton University Press, 1977), pp. 79–114, suggests Milton's indebtedness to, as well as his radical departure from, the usages of medieval typology.

13. The epic is, of course, a notoriously syncretic genre, even when it aspires above "th' Aonian Mount," and Raphael's discourse on astronomy (*PL* 8.66–178) offers some evidence of Milton's occasional willingness to entertain mutually irreconcilable hypotheses. On the question of philosophical syncretism see Michael Lieb, "Milton and the Metaphysics of Form," *Studies in Philology* 71 (1974): 206–24, who traces Milton's attempt to reconcile Aristotelian and Platonic conceptions of form.

14. St. Thomas Aquinas, *Theological Texts*, ed. and trans. Thomas Gilby (London: Oxford University Press, 1955), pp. 349, 350, 354, and 368; emphases added. The texts cited are *Summa Theologica* 3a.1x.2; *de Articulis Fidei et Sacramentis Ecclesiae* 2; IV *Contra Gentes* 56; and *Summa Theologica* 3a.1xxv.1.

15. Besides restricting both their mode of operation and their significance, Milton reduces the number of sacraments from seven to two, Baptism and Communion: "the other things which the Papists call sacraments . . . are not really sacraments at all" (p. 560). And he is skeptical about the term *sacrament* itself: "I do not see why much trouble should be taken to establish the precise meaning of the word when it does not even occur in the Bible" (p. 561).

16. In *Christian Doctrine* 1.7 Milton argues that all things "were made not out of nothing but out of matter," a substance which must have "originated from God at some point in time" (p. 307). Milton's materialism has been thoroughly explored by William B. Hunter, Jr., in "Milton's Materialistic Life Principle," *Journal of English and Germanic Philology* 45 (1946): 68–76, and "Milton's Power of Matter," *Journal of the History of Ideas* 13 (1952): 551–62.

17. A little later Milton is even more explicit: after the body of Christ "has been driven through all the stomach's filthy channels, it shoots it out—one shudders even to mention it—into the latrine" (p. 560).

18. *De Doctrina Christiana* 1.7; *Works*, 15: 18, 20, 22. Milton argues that God

created the world, not out of nothing, but out of his own substance: *Actio enim et passio relata cum sint, nullumque agens extra se possit agere, nisi sit quod pati queat, materia nimirum, Deus ex nihilo creare hunc mundum videtur non potuisse.* . . . *Materialis igitur causa erit Deus aut nihil.* . . . *Materia . . . et forma velut causae internae rem ipsam constituunt.* . . . *Materia . . . substantia erat, nec aliunde quam ex fonte omnis substantiae derivanda.* "Since matter and form, activity and passivity, are interdependent, and since no agency can act externally except upon some potential, such as matter, God could not have created the world out of nothing. . . . Therefore, the material cause is either God or nothing. . . . Matter and form are the internal causes of any existent thing and thus constitute the thing itself. . . . Matter is a *substance*, and not to be derived but from the source of every substance, which is God." Hunter, "Milton's Power of Matter," has shown that Milton's ideas of potency *(ex potentia materia)* and relative passivity are derived from Aristotle's conception of matter as potential form. The δύναμις, or potentiality, of matter is not mere passivity, it is rather the capability of being actualized by the ἐνέργεια of form. The point here, of course, is that matter and form, the internal causes of every existing thing, constitute a single substance. In the fifth chapter of the treatise Milton argues analogously that the Father and the Son, though not coessential, are consubstantial; see Hunter, "Further Definitions: Milton's Theological Vocabulary," in *Bright Essence*, pp. 15–25.

19. See *De Doctrina Christiana* 1.7; *Works*, 15: 22: *materia indigesta modo et incomposita, quam Deus postea digessit et ornavit.* Carey's translation renders Milton's syntax: "It was in a confused and disordered state at first, but afterwards God made it ordered and beautiful" (*CPW*, 6: 308). But Sumner's translation is closer to the metaphoric structure of Milton's Latin: "though at first confused and formless, being afterwards adorned and digested into order by the hand of God" (*Works*, 15: 23; emphasis added).

20. J. B. Broadbent, *Some Graver Subject: An Essay on "Paradise Lost"* (London: Chatto & Windus, 1960), pp. 207, 210.

21. Ibid., p. 210.

22. Madsen, *From Shadowy Types to Truth*, pp. 89, 87.

23. Broadbent, *Some Graver Subject*, p. 203.

24. On Spenser's combination of typological and Neoplatonic symbolism, see Angus Fletcher, *The Prophetic Moment: An Essay on Spenser* (Chicago: University of Chicago Press, 1971).

25. Medieval typology is, of course, *sacramental* in precisely the sense I intend, even though *allegoria* is an extension of the literal sense rather than its incarnation. On the inherent realism of Medieval typology, see, for example, Erich Auerbach's seminal essay, "Typological Symbolism in Medieval Literature," in *American Critical Essays on "The Divine Comedy,"* ed. Robert J. Clements (New York: New York University Press, 1967), pp. 104–13. Madsen argues, however, that Milton "creates his own types" (p. 82), and that their basis is wholly spiritual rather than historical.

26. B. Rajan, *"Paradise Lost" and the Seventeenth-Century Reader* (New York: Chatto & Windus, 1948), p. 35, has suggested that differences between the *Christian Doctrine* and *Paradise Lost* are "eventually due to differences in the media and aims of expository prose and epic poetry." C. A. Patrides, *"Paradise Lost* and the Language of Theology," in *Bright Essence*, pp. 171–72, argues an even more radical disjunction between poetry and dogma: "the treatise represents such an abortive venture into theology that Milton was forced drastically to alter his approach in

*Paradise Lost.*" In the epic Milton was finally able to resolve the intractable problems of the treatise because he adopted "a language whose center of gravity is the 'model' or—depending on the dictates of our particular critical vocabulary—the image, the metaphor, the symbol or the archetype, the emblem or the icon, perhaps even parabolic language and possibly 'myth.' "

27. See Maurice Kelley, *This Great Argument: A Study of Milton's "De Doctrina Christiana" as a Gloss upon "Paradise Lost"* (Princeton, N.J.: Princeton University Press, 1941). In his introduction to the treatise in *Complete Prose Works,* 6:103–16, Kelley reiterates his belief that "the treatise and the epic may . . . be assumed to be synchronous works that express in two different forms and manners the same body of religious beliefs" (p. 109). Kelley's reading of the treatise itself has not gone unchallenged, and his claim for the essential unanimity of the two works is surely exaggerated, but the basic validity of his approach is assumed even by his severest critics. Both Hunter and Patrides concede that "the prose treatise resolves certain doctrinal uncertainties in the poem" (p. 110).

28. Milton's claim is carefully hedged: *"Hesperian* Fables true, / If true, here only."* He acknowledges the possibility that his representation of Paradise is not absolutely accurate in detail; Eden is, however, a literal place as well as a metaphor, so that the truth of Scripture *actualizes* the imaginations of pagan poets.

29. Samuel Taylor Coleridge, *The Statesman's Manual,* in *The Complete Works of Samuel Taylor Coleridge,* ed. W. G. T. Shedd (New York: Harper & Brothers, 1875) p. 437.

30. Aquinas, *Summa Theologica* 3a.lxxv.4; *Theological Texts,* p. 370.

31. There is also some agreement on the question of sacramental significance. As C. A. Patrides has pointed out, in *Milton and the Christian Tradition,* p. 218, both Catholics and Protestants share Augustine's view that a sacrament is "the visible sign of an invisible grace"—*signum visibile gratiae invisibilis.* Compare Aquinas, *de Articulis Fidei et Sacramentis Ecclesiae* 2 (n. 3 above): *figura visibilis gratiae invisibilis;* and Milton, *Works,* 16:164: *signum visibile.*

32. Aquinas, *Summa Theologica* 3a.lx.6, ad 2; *Theological Texts,* pp. 351–52. See also *de Articulis Fidei et Sacramentis Ecclesiae* 2; *Theological Texts,* p. 350: Christ "is the Word made flesh, and as his flesh was sanctified and given sanctifying virtue because of the Word united to it, so sacramental things are sanctified and have sanctifying virtue because of the words uttered in them. A word, says Augustine, comes to the elements, and they become a sacrament. *[super Joannem Tract.* LXXX, on xv.3; *Patrologia Latinae* XXXV, 1840.]. Hence these sanctifying words are called the form of the sacraments, and the sanctified elements the matter."

33. Aquinas, *de Articulis Fidei et Sacramentis Ecclesiae* 2; *Theological Texts,* p. 350. Aquinas himself anticipates one of the chief Protestant arguments against a literal-minded or "magical" understanding of sacramental efficacy, that the mere act in itself *(opus operatum)* is neither a sufficient nor a necessary cause of grace: if a communicant "receives the sacrament for outward show without his heart being prepared: he receives the sacrament, but not its effect . . . . Conversely, there are others who never take a sacrament and yet receive its effects from their devotion and desire" (ibid., p. 351).

34. *Works,* 16:204, 198: *sacramentum nihil aliud nisi obsignatio, vel potius repraesentatio* and *tropus sive usus loquendi figuratus.*

35. Kelley, *CPW,* 6:555, compares Wollebius, *The Abridgement of Christian Divinitie* (London, 1650), 1:22, pp. 144–45: "From the union and relation of the thing signified, with the signe; there ariseth a sacramental phrase or speech, in which

the thing signified is predicated of the signe: In this manner of speech is expressed what these outward signs signifie, rather than what they are in themselves, or of their own nature."

36. There is a nice ambiguity in the last phrase. Its obvious meaning is "[such] as may express them best," that is, by choosing those visible likenesses which most closely approximate invisible reality. But the phrase might just as well mean "since [that is] the best way to express spiritual forms: viz., corporally." The latter reading especially implies—as the passage as a whole seems to do—that language is the sacramental embodiment of thought, as body is the expression of spirit.

37. Barfield, *Saving the Appearances*, p. 89.

38. *Of Reformation Touching Church-Discipline in England (CPW*, 1:520).

39. *The Reason of Church-government Urg'd against Prelaty*, 2.2 *(CPW*, 1:828).

40. Milton continues: "what he gave was the heavenly and spiritual bread which had come down from heaven. It was not the earthly bread, which had been born from the virgin and which, had he merely given his flesh, he would have given, but a bread which was, so to speak, more heavenly than the manna itself, and which *he who eats shall live for ever*, [John], vi.58."

41. Samuel Taylor Coleridge, *Aids to Reflection*, ed. T. Ashe (London: G. Bell, 1892), p. 136, draws an analogous distinction between symbols, which are "always *taut*egorical, that is, expressing the same subject but with a difference" and "metaphors and similitudes, that are always *alle*gorical, that is, expressing a different subject but with a resemblance." See also *Biographia Literaria*, ed. J. Shawcross (Oxford: Oxford University Press, 1954), 2:209n, where Coleridge speaks of "the allegorizing fancy of the *modern*, that still *striving* to project the inward, contradistinguishes itself from the seeming ease with which the poetry of the ancients reflects the world without."

42. *Pearl*, 11. 1209–9, in *"Pearl" and "Sir Gawain and the Green Knight*," ed. A. C. Cawley (New York: Dutton, 1962).

43. Paul Piehler, *The Visionary Landscape: A Study in Medieval Allegory* (London: Edward Arnold, 1971), pp. 152–53.

44. *Christian Doctrine* 1.24 *(CPW*, 6:499; *Works*, 16:58): *participatio per spiritum.* Milton concludes that, from the "union and communion [of the regenerate] with the Father and with Christ, and among the members of Christ's body themselves . . . there comes into being that mystic body, THE INVISIBLE CHURCH, the head of which is Christ" (p. 499). One would be tempted to read such references to the mystical body (cf. Romans 12:4–5, 1 Corinthians 12:12–13, 27) as instances of sacramental participation, were it not for Milton's insistence that our participation in "Christ's gifts and merits" is always a consequence of our *conscious* regeneration. His repeated strictures against merely implicit faith press directly on this point, as does his argument against infant baptism: "infants are not fit for baptism" because "they cannot believe or undertake an obligation" (p. 545); "this calls for the intelligence and faith of a grown-up man" (p. 546).

45. Barfield, *Saving the Appearances*, p. 172.

46. Madsen, *From Shadowy Types to Truth*, p. 82.

47. *Of Reformation (CPW*, 1:520).

48. Barfield, *Saving the Appearances*, p. 172.

49. *Christian Doctrine* 1.7; *Works*, 15:22, 48: *materia . . . [potentia modo et] indigesta . . . et incomposita, quam Deus postea digessit et ornavit*, and *omnem certe formam . . . ex potentia materiae produci omnes fere consentiunt.* Oddly enough, Carey follows Sumner's mistranslation of the latter passage: "form . . . is produced

by the power of matter" *(CPW,* 6:322; *Works,* 15:49). Hunter, "Milton's Power of Matter," p. 551, has shown that the phrase *ex potentia materiae* means "from the potentiality of matter," in accordance with Aristotle's idea that matter is potentiality (see n. 18 above).

50. Augustine, *De Civitate Dei* 7.32, in *The City of God,* trans. Marcus Dods (New York: Modern Library, 1950), p. 238: "The mystery of eternal life, even from the beginning of the human race, was, by certain signs and sacraments suitable to the times . . . signified and fore-announced."

51. In *Christian Doctrine* 1.2 *(CPW,* 6:133), Milton argues that we ought "to form an image of God in our minds which corresponds to his representation and description of himself in the sacred writings . . . not as he really is but in such a way as will make him conceivable to us"; that is, "we ought to form just such a mental image of him as he, in bringing himself within the limits of our undestanding, wishes us to form."

PART II

*The Philosophical Dimension*

# "The Scholastick Grosnesse of Barbarous ages": The Question of the Humanism of Milton's Understanding of Virtue

Paul M. Dowling

THE argument that Milton's thought is more akin to that of Thomas Aquinas than to that of Aristotle certainly defies the perception many readers have of Milton. In a number of his works Milton appears to reject the scholasticism of the Middle Ages and to embrace the humanism of classical antiquity. Cases in point are his most popular prose works, *Of Education* and *Areopagitica*. The first describes a course of "virtuous and noble Education"[1] based, by Milton's reckoning, on rejection of the scholastic influence on contemporary English schools and on imitation of the educational practice of classical antiquity. The title of the present paper, which is drawn from that treatise, seems to convey Milton's attitude toward scholasticism and the age that produced it. In another place in the same work Milton quotes approvingly from the classical work on virtuous education, Aristotle's *Nicomachean Ethics*. The other prose work argues that Parliament ought to recall a law licensing books because licensing hinders rather than promotes virtue and truth.[2] The Greek title itself, *Areopagitica*, is from an oration about virtuous education by the classical writer Isocrates. In one place in his own oration Milton appears to criticize Thomas Aquinas, the scholastic par excellence, as an inferior teacher of virtue. But despite these indications of Milton's intellectual kinship, Milton's thinking in both works is more scholastic and less humanistic than is frequently acknowledged. An indication of Milton's true kinship is that, on the issue crucial for both works of the meaning of virtue, Milton is closer to Aquinas than to Aristotle.

We need, then, to see briefly what each of these authors understands by the term *virtue*.

Aristotle discusses the subject of virtue in the ten books of his *Nicomachean Ethics*.[3] He uses the word *virtue* to mean some form of excellence or goodness, and he discusses two kinds of virtue, moral in the first half of the work and intellectual in the other half. Aristotle's criterion for what is excellent or good is the fact that it is praised. "Praise belongs to virtue," Aristotle says in the first book of the *Ethics* (1.12.1101b32033); and he ends that book by saying "praiseworthy dispositions we term virtue" (1.13.1103a10). This criterion leads to different degrees of precision in discussing the two kinds of virtue. For, since the praise that moral virtue receives varies from one society to another and is less discriminating than that which intellectual virtue receives, the subject of moral virtue admits considerably more variation and less precision than that of intellectual virtue. Since it is Aristotle's principle not to demand greater precision than the subject admits, the discussion of the moral virtues in the first half of the work is less precise than that of the intellectual virtues in the second half of the work. For, Aristotle argues, "it is the mark of an educated mind to expect that amount of exactness in each kind which the nature of the particular subject admits" (1.3.23–25). Hence, in the context of introducing the moral virtues, Aristotle says that since his subject has "many variations and errors . . . we must . . . be content if, in dealing with subjects and starting from premises thus uncertain, we succeed in presenting a broad outline of the truth" (1.3.1094b14–16, 19–21).

I might illustrate Aristotle's methodological principle of seeking only the degree of precision appropriate to the subject matter by an analogy he uses in the *Ethics* (1.7.1098a28–35). He notes the difference between the degree of precision required for the angle used by a carpenter and that used by a geometrician. The angle used by a carpenter is imprecise from the point of view of the geometrician. But the carpenter's angle is sufficiently precise for all practical purposes. We all— geometricians as well as others—live in houses and sit on chairs and at tables made with carpenter's angles. In fact, if carpenters insisted upon the degree of precision required for an angle in geometry, there would be very few houses, chairs, and tables. Analogously, the degree of precision required to discuss the intellectual virtues is inappropriate to Aristotle's discussion of the moral virtues. In fact, to insist upon this inappropriate degree of precision would destroy the phenomena of morality.

Aristotle's maintaining of the moral phenomena as they come to light in praise and blame can be seen in two instances to be relevant to Milton. At the beginning of Book 3 Aristotle defines the involuntary as that which takes place under compulsion (when the moving principle is outside the agent) and owing to ignorance. The importance of understanding the involuntary is obvious in a discussion of virtue, since actions that are involuntary cannot be truly virtuous. It might be observed that many acts of what Aristotle calls moral virtue, for instance, acts of courage or of temperance, to some extent partake of the involuntary. Such deeds are posited out of habits inculcated by the mores of a particular society. Aristotle, however, does not make such an observation because the degree of precision implied is inappropriate: it would destroy these acts as forms of excellence coming to light in praise. In the chapter in question, Aristotle merely says that "voluntary actions [are those] for which praise and blame are given" (3.1.1109b31).

Aristotle's preserving the moral phenomena is also evident in his use of the term προαίρεσις or choice. Again the importance of understanding choice in a study of ethics is obvious. Only an agent who is fully aware of his alternatives can be said in the most precise sense to have made a choice of virtue. In the first half of the work, however, Aristotle is deliberately and in principle imprecise about the extent of rational awareness that is requisite for the moral virtues. Do acts of moral virtue, for instance, require the agent to possess the intellectual virtue of prudence or practical wisdom? Aristotle is ambiguous. In 2.6 he says that the virtuous mean in which moral virtue consists is "determined by a principle, that is as the prudent man would determine it" (1107a1). But does the agent himself have to be prudent to determine such a principle? Aristotle does not say. Again, at 3.2 Aristotle defines προαίρεσις with similar ambiguity as "a voluntary action preceded by deliberation, since choice involves reasoning and some process of thought" (1112a16). Which process of thought Aristotle does not say, although in an earlier context discussing choice he remarks that "for the possession of the virtues, knowledge is of little or no avail" (2.4. 1105a4–5). But in the second half of the *Ethics*, in the context of the discussion of the intellectual virtues, Aristotle clarifies his earlier ambiguity. In 6.14 he says that true προαίρησις, true choice, requires prudence. True virtue cannot exist without it, although what he calls natural virtue can. Hence in the more precise sense the ethical virtues cannot exist in isolation from the intellectual. But to insist on this precision in the context of the moral virtues would involve a contradiction with the principle of defining virtue by the imprecise standards of praise. For (to take but one example) many of the men who are praised for courageous acts in war for their country do not possess the rare intellectual virtues.

If Aristotle in his *Nicomachean Ethics* distinguishes different degrees of precision appropriate to moral virtue on the one hand and to intellectual virtue on the other, Thomas Aquinas in his *Commentary on the Nicomachean Ethics* and his *Summa Theologica* fails to note this distinction and hence insists on the same degree of precision in discussing both kinds of virtue.[4] Aquinas's great work was the attempt to harmonize reason and faith. Assuming that there could be no unresolvable conflict or contradiction between the two, Thomas presented, especially in his various commentaries on the works of Aristotle, a synthesis of pagan reason in the form of Aristotle's philosophy and Judeo-Christian faith in the form of the Bible. As we shall see, one indication of the problematic status of this assumption is that Thomas seeks for greater precision in the moral phenomena than Aristotle thought appropriate.

The most telling way in which Thomas achieves greater precision in his moral teaching than Aristotle is through attributing to Aristotle his own Christian teaching on conscience and natural law. In the *Summa Theologica* (1–2.94.1) Thomas argues that there is a natural habit of the practical intellect called conscience (or, more technically, συντήρησις), analogous to the natural habit of the speculative intellect. Although Aristotle does include among his intellectual virtues a natural habit of the speculative intellect called intuitive reason (νους) he nowhere mentions Thomas's analogous conscience or συντήρησις. Furthermore, Thomas argues in both the *Summa* and in his *Commentary on the Ethics* that conscience or συντήρησις intuitively knows certain principles of what he calls natural law. Nearly all men everywhere, Thomas claims, naturally know an extensive and unchangeable code of right and just things deduced from these principles, almost in the manner in which a system of geometrical theorems is deduced from axioms and postulates. This teaching of Thomas about natural law *(lex)* is a distortion of Aristotle's teaching about natural right (δίκαιον) Aristotle teaches that natural right is a part of political right and that men take their moral bearings by the laws and customs (νόμος) of their particular political society. "Although there is such a thing as natural justice or right," says Aristotle, "all rules of justice are variable" (*NE* 5.7.1134b29–30). The true Aristotelian equivalent of conscience is the sense of shame that well-nurtured men feel at the thought of committing deeds that violate the ethical norms encouraged by their particular society. But the sense of shame, far from reflecting a natural or universal law, reflects the mores of a particular society. To refer once more to Aristotle's analogy of the angle of the carpenter and that of the geometrician, Thomas's teaching on conscience and natural law attributes to the practical carpenter a degree of precision that Aristotle thinks appropriate only to the speculative geometrician.

Thomas carefully follows Aristotle's teaching on habit without commenting on the extent to which this teaching implies a diminution of the voluntary and thereby of the truly virtuous in acts of moral virtue. The voluntary requires that the moving principle be within the agent. In the case of moral virtues, the moving principle is to some extent in the mores of a particular political society established by a founder or lawgiver (νομοθέτης). While the founder or establisher of these mores may act voluntarily and thereby virtuously, the citizens formed by the mores of his society would seem to posit acts of moral virtue with diminished volition and thereby diminished virtue. Are acts of moral virtue, then, truly virtuous? Aristotle remains silent on this question and thereby does not insist upon a degree of precision that would destroy the phenomena he is studying. Aristotle suggests this line of reasoning, however, by noting the connection in Greek between the word for moral (ἠθικός) anu that for habit (ἦθος): "moral or ethical virtue is the product of habit, and has indeed derived its name, with a slight variation of form, from that word" (*NE* 2.1.1103a17–19). Thomas simply reproduces the equivalent similarity of words in his Latin: "moralis virtus fit ex more, id est ex consuetudine," or, "moral virtue is produced from mores, that is from custoin or habit."[5] And Thomas continues with a paraphrase of Aristotle on the lawgiver's educative task: "Legislators make men virtuous by habituating them to virtuous work by means of statutes, rewards, and punishments. Such ought to be the aim of every legislator—in fact he who does not succeed in this fails in lawmaking. It is precisely in this way that a good [regime] differs from a bad one" (251). Thomas does not register here any question about a tension between this teaching and that about the voluntary.

But on the question of choice (προαίρεσις), Thomas attributes greater intellectual awareness to moral virtue than does Aristotle. Aristotle's initial definition of choice, as was previously noted, is appropriately imprecise: choice is "voluntary action preceded by deliberation, since choice involves reasoning and some process of thought" (*NE*3.2.1112a15–17). Thomas remarks that "choice itself must be accompanied by an act of reason and intellect" (457). But Thomas means by "act of reason and intellect" something more precise than what Aristotle at this stage of his argument intends. Thomas means to impute to the passage in Book 3 the precise distinction between natural virtue and true virtue which Aristotle withholds until the end of Book 6. Thomas makes this retroactive application of the later distinction clear in the first sentence of his commentary on 6.13: "After the Philosopher has shown that prudence cannot exist without moral virtue, he now shows that moral virtue cannot exist without prudence" (1275). But it is Aristotle's position in the first half of his work that moral virtue can indeed exist without prudence.

For Aquinas, then, although moral virtue springs from habit, it requires the presence of the intellectual virtue of prudence. The point of agreement between this understanding and that of Aristotle is that moral virtue is habitual. This agreement is illustrated by the fact that both maintain that the state they call continence is not a virtue, because, although the continent man imitates the actions of the temperate with respect to food, drink, and sex, he does so not out of habit but, as Aristotle says, "knowing that his appetites are bad, refuses on account of his rational principle to follow them" (*NE*7.1.1145b13–14). In his *Commentary* Aquinas follows Aristotle, saying that "the temperate man will not be continent, nor the continent man temperate, for the man who is completely temperate does not have evil desires in any vehemence" (1320). The temperate man has so habituated himself to temperate deeds that he no longer has the evil desires the continent man struggles with.

That Milton's understanding of virtue is closer to Aquinas's than to Aristotle's can be attributed to the fact that they are both Christians who, despite doctrinal differences, share the problematic assumption that classical reasoning and Christian belief can be harmonized. Milton's titling his work after a classical oration on the powers of the legislator over virtuous education is one sign of this assumption. Another is that Milton claims to agree with Plato on the powers of the legislator over virtuous education and attempts to prove this agreement with parallel arguments from what he calls "the manner of God and of nature" (2:526–28, esp. 528). However, the extent to which faith dictates to reason in Milton's understanding of virtue can be seen in his treatment of habit, choice, and temperance.

Milton's attitude toward habit is emphatically negative. Many of the most memorable and impassioned passages from the *Areopagitica* attack habit. Such is the following, which argues that Christians must transcend habit, custom, and prejudice because

> our faith and knowledge thrives by exercise, as well as our limbs and complexion. Truth is compared in Scripture to a streaming fountain; if her waters flow not in a perpetual progression, they sicken into a muddy pool of conformity and tradition. A man may be a heretic in the truth; and if he believe things only because his Pastor says so, or the Assembly so determines, without knowing other reason, though his belief be true, yet the very truth he holds, becomes his heresy. (2:543)

Milton emphatically subordinates habit to reason as the foundation for virtue because, as he explains most clearly in the *Areopagitica*, virtue sustained by habit is not true virtue: the very lack of awareness associated with merely habitual virtue prevents the trial by vice needed to purify the soul of original sin and gain personal immortality. In a famous and moving period from that speech Milton rejects a virtue that flees from combat with vice: "I cannot praise a fugitive and cloistered virtue, unexercised and unbreathed, that never sallies out and sees her adversary, but slinks out of the race, where the immortal garland is to be run for, not without dust and heat" (2:515). Such a virtue is "but a blank virtue, not a pure; her whiteness is but an excremental whiteness" (2:515–16). Milton's reason for rejecting such a virtue as superficial depends upon Christian revelation: "We bring not innocence into the world, we bring impurity much rather; that which purifies us is trial, and trial is by what is contrary" (2:515).

Milton's faith and the consequences he draws from it not only demand a high level of awareness in the practice of virtue; they also place crucial restrictions on the laws and the prudence of the legislator. He is prevented from establishing the kind of paternalistic care for the *mores* that Aristotle and even Aquinas approve of because such care would interfere with achieving the transpolitical good of immortality. Milton makes this latter point clear again in the *Areopagitica* while justifying a distinction between areas where the coercive powers of law can operate and those where only persuasion should work.

> If every action which is good, or evil in man at ripe years were to be under pittance, and prescription, and compulsion, what were virtue but a name, what praise could be then due to well-doing, what gramercy to be sober, just or continent? many there be that complain of divine Providence for suffering *Adam* to transgress, foolish tongues! when God gave him reason, he gave him freedom to choose, for reason is but choosing; he had been else a mere artificial *Adam*, such an *Adam* as he is in the motions. . . . God . . . left him free, set before him a provoking object, ever almost in his eyes; herein consisted his merit, herein the right of his reward, the praise of his abstinence. Wherefore did he create passions within us, pleasures round about us, but that these rightly tempered are the very ingredients of virtue? (2:527)

Milton bases his understanding of this distinction between areas of compulsion and those of persuasion on Christian revelation. He maintains that there must be sufficient freedom to choose in civil society so that eternal salvation is truly merited because derived from responsibility. Virtue is nothing but a name unless it springs from free and reasonable choosing. God left men free to moderate their passions and the world's pleasures to virtuous conduct. The licenser would make man a mere puppet ("a mere artificial *Adam*"); he would reduce him below the level required by Christian responsibility.

In view of Milton's stance on habit, it is easy to see what his stance on choice, Aristotle's προαίρησις, must be. Far from allowing choice to be located anywhere along a spectrum of possible mental states, as Aristotle does, Milton must limit choice for mature and educated men to reasoned choice. Of course Milton realizes that the choice of the immature is not yet reasonable. The freedom from licensing that *Areopagitica* proposes is for man who is "mature," "grown," "at ripe years" (2:513,527). To benefit from such freedom in maturity, he should have the kind of virtuous education in his youth described by *Of Education*. And that education places certain constraints on the youth so that he will not acquire "ill habits" (2:414). It is only once students have been through a good part of this education that "years and good general precepts will have furnished them with that act of reason which in *Ethics* is called *Proairesis:* that they may with some judgment contemplate upon moral good and evil" (2:396). But a further, possible implication of this sentence is that fully matured, educated men exercise a προαίρησις, a choosing, which can be defined as an "act of reason."

One's impression that Milton equates choice or *proairesis* with an act of reason is strengthened by considering the meaning of the *Areopagitica*'s pivotal phrase, "reason is but choosing" (2:527). In certain contexts in the *Areopagitica* Milton means by this phrase to define reason: unless all manner of opinions are allowed freedom to be argued, unless in other words the licenser is eliminated, reason is not truly operative. It is not sufficient that one's belief be true to be reasonable; for, if a man has not arrived at it reasonably by considering all the alternatives, "though his belief be true, yet the very truth he holds becomes a heresy" (2:543). But insofar as the phrase defines reason, it also defines choice; for it is characteristic of definitions, according to Milton's *Art of Logic,* that they be convertible.[6] So "reason is but choosing" can be converted (with the qualifying "but" reworded but unchanged in meaning) into "that only is choosing which is reasonable." In Aristotelian terms, Milton is saying that the moral virtues cannot exist in isolation from the intellectual virtues. Truly virtuous choosing requires the presence of reasoned choosing. Obviously this definition of choice is closer to that of Aquinas than to that of Aristotle.

But however close Milton is to Thomas on the issue of choice, his understanding of virtue still differs from Thomas's. And this difference accounts for the passage from *Areopagitica* where Milton criticizes Aquinas as an inferior teacher of virtue.[7] The context for this passage is a distinction between true and false virtue.

> That virtue therefore which is but a youngling in the contemplation of evill, and knows not the utmost that vice promises to her followers, and rejects it, is but a blank vertue, not a pure; her whitenesse is but an excrementall whitenesse; Which is the reason why our sage and serious Poet *Spencer*, whom I dare be known to think a better teacher than *Scotus* or *Aquinas*, describing true temperance under the person of *Guion*, brings him in with his palmer through the cave of Mammon, and the bowr of earthly blisse that he might see and know, and yet abstain. (2: 515–16)

The context suggests that the "true temperance" that Spenser describes "under the person of Guion" is an example of that virtue which knows "the utmost that vice promises her followers, and rejects it." Rather than remaining within the cloister created by licensing, true or Spenserian temperance goes forth "into the regions of sin and falsity . . . by reading all manner of tractats [sic], and hearing all manner of reason" (2: 517). Spenser is a "better teacher" because he describes "true temperance" by bringing Guyon in with his palmer (the allegorical figure for practical reason) so that Guyon "might see and know, and yet abstain." In the light of this interpretation, even Milton's mistake (as editors and critics since Sirluck have termed it) about Spenser makes sense. For in *The*

*Fairie Queene* itself, Spenser allows Guyon to face the temptations of Mammon's cave without his palmer because he believes that these temptations can be overcome by Guyon's habitual temperance alone without the guidance of reason or right reason. But, as we have seen, Milton rejects a virtue founded merely on habit. So Milton's mistake can be viewed as Milton's rewriting of Spenser's narrative to fit his own understanding of virtue.

In effect, Miltonic temperance resembles Aristotelian-Thomistic continence in eschewing habit in favor of the conscious effort to overcome temptation (to "see and know, and yet abstain"). Aquinas, then, is an inferior teacher because, in retaining Aristotle's hegemony of temperance over continence, he failed to teach "true temperance," a virtue based on the principle that trial by evil desires must purify the soul of the impurity of original sin in order to merit personal immortality.

By way of conclusion, we should return to Milton's status as a humanist and his relation to Aquinas. If by a humanist we mean someone whose conclusions are based on reason rather than faith or revealed dogmas, it is difficult to see how Milton's understanding of virtue qualifies him for that title. For in his presentation of this matter the triumph of faith over reason is clear. And this triumph points to Milton's profound kinship with Aquinas, a kinship partially obscured by their disagreements over habit, the lawgiver, and temperance. Despite these disagreements, Milton shares with Aquinas a faith in the divine perspective on moral matters that makes his understanding of virtue theological rather than humanistic.

## Notes

This essay was drafted during a National Endowment for the Humanities Seminar for the Summer of 1976 under Professor Earl Miner of Princeton University. The author wishes to state that, although his 1976 thesis still seems accurate and helpful as far as it goes, it would be useful to place *Areopagitica*'s theory of virtue into the larger context of Milton's rhetoric in that work.

1. Ernest Sirluck, ed., *Complete Prose Works of John Milton*, gen. ed., Don M. Wolfe (New Haven, Conn.: Yale University Press, 1959), 2: 376; hereafter both Milton works will be cited in parenthesis by volume and page number, with spelling modernized.

2. While it is true that the *Areopagitica* speaks at least as much in favor of liberty as of virtue, it should be noted that (as Arthur Barker says) "the *Areopagitica* is a magnificently eloquent appeal for a particular kind of liberty, for Christian liberty in indifferent things. 'The adjectives involve significant reservations." See *Milton and the Puritan Dilemma* (Toronto: University of Toronto Press, 1942), p. 97. Among those reservations are that Milton thinks of liberty as both a means toward virtue and, in its most exalted sense, as the possession of true virtue. See Barker, p. 182, and *A Second Defence of The English People* in Don M. Wolfe, ed., *Complete Prose Works of John Milton*, 4: 1.679–82. The difference between Barker's interpretation of *Areopagitica* and my own is in part one of terminology due to Barker's Puritan perspective and my classical and medieval one, one that Barker acknowledges he does not emphasize (pp. xxi, 139, 183, and 213). It should be added, however, that my perspective has led me to doubt the usefulness of Barker's references to Milton's rational humanism.

3. H. Rackham, trans., *Aristotle, The Nicomachean Ethics,* The Loeb Classical Library (Cambridge, Mass.: Harvard University Press, 1926); hereafter cited in parentheses by book and Stephanus number.

4. The following discussion of the ways Thomas Aquinas modifies Aristotelian ethics is indebted to Harry V. Jaffa, *Thomism and Aristotelianism* (Chicago: University of Chicago Press), 1952.

5. *In Decem Libros Ethicorum Aristotelis Ad Nicomachum Expositio*, ed. P. Fr. Raymundi M. Spiazzi (Rome: Marietti, 1949), p. 247. Hereafter the citations in parenthesis are to C. I. Litzinger, trans., *Commentary on the Nicomachean Ethics* (Chicago: Henry Regnery Company, 1964).

6. John Milton, *Artis Logicae Plenior Institutio*, trans. Allan H. Gilbert, in *The Works of John Milton* (New York: Columbia University, 1935), 11: 261–63 (Bk. 7, chap. 30).

7. In the following paragraphs I follow the interpretation of Ernest Sirluck, "Milton revises *The Faerie Queene,*" *Modern Philology* 48 (1950): 90–96. We differ only in the following: Sirluck sees Milton's divergence from Aristotle as Ciceronian, whereas I view it as Christian. For the suggestion that Milton's rejection of habitual temperance and habit itself finds support in Christianity, I am indebted to the discussion of continence in Jaffa, *Thomism and Aristotelianism*, pp. 59–61. For an interpretation differing from Sirluck's in arguing that Milton is thinking of different poetic traditions rather than of ethical persuasions, see Raymond G. Schoen, "Milton and Spenser's Cave of Mammon Episode," *Philological Quarterly* 54 (1975): 684–89.

## [ 4 ]
# Sway and Subjection: Natural Causation and the Portrayal of Paradise in the Summa Theologica and Paradise Lost

Ellen Goodman

IT is not surprising that Miltonists have given little attention to St. Thomas Aquinas. They are well aware of Milton's Puritan and Ramist tendencies and of his objections to Catholicism and scholastic philosophy. They know, too, that Milton mentioned Aquinas by name only when he proposed that Spenser was the "better teacher." But Joseph Duncan, in *Milton's Earthly Paradise,* raises an issue about Milton and Aquinas that warrants closer attention. Duncan notes that Thomas's views of paradise were still widely respected in the seventeenth century, even among English Protestants, and that Milton, too, accepted many Thomistic ideas about the state of innocence.[1] These remarks invite further inquiry into the relationships among Thomas's vision of Eden, the views of Protestants, and the poetic portrayal of paradise in Milton's epic. What commends such inquiry to readers of *Paradise Lost* is that it may clarify the kind of paradise Milton designed and the patterns of thought that underlie his art.

One feature of Aquinas's treatment of paradise particularly worth our attention is his use of the concept of natural causation. By synthesizing Christian theology and Aristotelian

philosophy, Aquinas is commonly recognized to have developed a systematic Christian view of the operations and
interrelationships among parts of nature. This concept plays
an important role in his treatment of Eden in the *Summa
Theologica*. Such matters as the heat of the sun in Eden, the
preservative effects of the fruit of the tree of life, human
reproduction, and the usefulness of the creation of woman[2]
concern Aquinas in part because of his interest in relations of
cause and effect within the natural order. One reason that
Aquinas's rational, particularized paradise seems to Duncan
to resemble the literal, historical Eden of Renaissance in-
terpreters may be that they broadly accepted the Chris-
tianized theory of natural causation to which Aquinas had
contributed so much.

In order to suggest more precisely how Aquinas's conception of natural causation influenced his view of Eden, let me
summarize briefly the central features of this familiar theory.
The traditional notion of natural causation depended on the
proposition that parts of nature were arranged in a hierarchy
of active and passive agents. For Aquinas, as for Aristotle, the
main active agents in nature were the celestial bodies, whose
movements around the earth he considered to prompt all
earthly generation and corruption. The distinction between
active and passive principles of causation, superiors and subordinates in the hierarchy of causes, was heightened by the
notion that the stars were composed not of the earthly elements of fire, air, water, and earth, but of a fifth element
which made them fully actual forms, invulnerable to change
and hence impervious to the influence of other parts of nature. Together with their universal sway, the invulnerable
substance traditionally accorded to the stars served both to
stress their supremacy in matters of natural causation and also
to secure the regularity and orderliness of relationships and
processes throughout the natural world.

By means of the distinction between active and passive

agents of causation, nature as a whole became, for Aquinas, a series of interlocking tiers through which influence descended from higher agents to their subordinates. Acting on appropriate materials, the stars were though to cause the "spontaneous" generation of insects and other "imperfect" or asexual species and also to assist in sexual reproduction. Though human beings possessed free wills, their bodies, dispositions, and passions might be affected by patterns of celestial movement and influence.[3] In sexual reproduction the male was considered the active agent of causation and the female passive, providing the matter on which the male's active force worked to stimulate development. In the theory of natural causation, then, the relationships of sway and subjection that extended throughout the cosmos were mirrored in microcosm in human sexuality.

This view of natural causation, and particularly of the celestial bodies, vitally affects Aquinas's treatment of Eden. In essence, Aquinas envisions Eden as an enclave in which human beings would have been exempted from the more adverse conditions normally allocated to earthly things through their subjection to the influence of the stars. The ideal situation of Eden, he proposes, precluded the extremes of climate and weather conditions generally produced on earth through the movements of the stars. Moreover, the tree of life prevented physical corruption by restoring bodily vitality. Aquinas emphasizes the special adaptation of Eden to the well-being of humans by proposing that none of the animals would have lived there and by insisting that paradise would not have been exposed to even such temporary extremes as the heat caused by the sun's course over the equator.[4] Though he believes that people would have been subject to laws of causation in Eden, Aquinas designs an earthly paradise that exempts unfallen humanity from the difficult physical conditions into which Adam and Eve were banished after original sin.

Both Aquinas's view of Eden and his use of the theory of

natural causation depend on a third, complementary aspect of his thought, his view of the consequences of original sin. While he holds that original sin affected man and altered his relationships with other parts of nature, Aquinas considers the operations of the natural world itself as remaining unaffected by human disobedience. His restriction of the effects of original sin to the sphere of human activities is evident in his reading of the curse on Adam in Genesis 3:17. Aquinas takes this verse to read, "cursed is the earth in thy work," insisting that the earth was cursed only in relation to man's work and not in itself.[5] Such a reading simultaneously supports and is supported by Aquinas's view of natural causation, for the changeless influence of the stars assumes and assures the constancy of nature as a whole for the duration of time.

The radical way in which Protestants departed from this assessment of the effects of original sin has not been adequately appreciated or investigated. But such Protestant commentators as Luther and Calvin interpreted Genesis 3:17 quite differently from Aquinas, and in doing so they advanced a substantially different view of nature, of the state of innocence, and of the garden of Eden. Instead of finding man's work the subject of God's curse on Adam, Luther and Calvin took Genesis 3:17 to read "cursed is the earth on thy account" and "cursed is the earth for thy sake," respectively.[6] Together, Aquinas's reading of this verse and his view of natural causation articulate his sense of the unaltered goodness and order of nature during the course of postlapsarian history. In preferring a different reading of the curse, Luther and Calvin express a different—and a darker—vision of the natural world during "fallen" time. For them, original sin brought not only the Fall of Man but a corresponding degeneration in the whole of nature.

As they extended the consequences of original sin to nature as well as man, Luther and Calvin were simultaneously reassessing the state of innocence and the role of the earthly paradise. By making the Fall of Man the point of time at which adverse conditions and harmful phenomena were instituted in nature, they excluded from the original design of the creation various hardships, menaces, and difficulties that Aquinas had considered useful and proper parts of the creation as long as they did not impede man's prelapsarian happiness.[7] The idea that adversities entered the natural world because of original sin served for Luther and Calvin not only to explain the difficulties of earthly life after the Fall; it also permitted them to contain such adversities within "fallen" nature and hence to envision, before the Fall, an idyllic, exclusively beneficent, and purely harmonious world.[8] Paradoxically, then, the more pessimistic attitudes of Protestant commentators toward nature after Adam's Fall express also a more idealized view of nature before human disobedience. In finding that the consequences of original sin extended throughout nature, Luther and Calvin simultaneously expanded the prelapsarian state of innocence to include nature as well as man.

From this expansion flows another common feature of their views of the state of innocence. As Luther and Calvin developed the idea of an "unfallen" world—a notion quite alien to Thomistic thought—they also reinterpreted the significance of Eden. In Thomas's treatment, the paradisal qualities of man's prelapsarian life depended largely on the locale of the earthly paradise. As the original and proper home of humanity, Eden was, for Aquinas, categorically different from the rest of the earth, expressing man's unique position and providing appropriately for his welfare. Aquinas's identification of human innocence with the garden of Eden reflects his reliance on different sets of criteria for adjudging what is good and appropriate for man and what is good and appropriate for other creatures. When Luther and Calvin extended the state of innocence to embrace nature as well as man, Thomas's sharp distinction between the good of humanity and the good of nature was considerably reduced, and so, too, was the distinction between the earthly paradise and the larger earth. Eden remained a paradise in Protestant thought, but not an enclave against harms and hardships outside of its territorial boundaries. Instead, the earthly paradise was subordinated to the notion of an unfallen world, and Eden became the crowning glory of nature in a primordial "golden age," from which harms and hardships were excluded not territorially but temporally.[9]

A glance at Milton's treatment of the Fall and its aftermath in *Paradise Lost* suffices to show that Milton adheres to the views advanced by such Protestant commentators as Luther and Calvin. Milton's Son echoes the Protestant reading of Genesis 3:17 when he declares to Adam, "Curs'd is the ground for thy sake" (10.201)[10]—not "in thy work," as Aquinas had held. In Book 10, moreover, Milton shows the angels forcibly altering the course of the stars in punishment of human disobedience. The Protestant tenor of Milton's account of the Fall and its consequences for nature makes it reasonable to suppose that Milton also observes the general features of Protestant thought in portraying paradise and the world before the Fall.

Yet it is also clear, as Kester Svendsen abundantly demonstrates in *Milton and Science*,[11] that the traditional concept of natural causation provides an essential structure for Milton's thought and imagery in representing the natural world and the garden of Eden. Such a combination of Protestant with traditional, Thomistic patterns of thought is not particularly alarming, given the pervasive influence of the theory of natural causation. What distinguishes Milton's use of these two patterns of thought is the kind of synthesis he effects between them. Rather than simply joining a Thomistic theory of natural causation to a Protestant view of Eden and of the effects of original sin, Milton filters the Thomistic hierarchy of causes through the lens of a Protestant perspective. In the vision of

Eden and the unfallen world that results, both the Thomistic and the Protestant elements are bent and blended to create an original, highly coherent treatment of relationships between superiors and subordinates in the hierarchy of causes.

Milton's blending of Thomistic and Protestant patterns of thought appears most conspicuously in his exclusion of harmful influences from nature before the Fall. While stressing descriptions of natural causation in his portrayal of unfallen nature, Milton persistently calibrates the processes he depicts to the standard of pure harmony found in Protestant treatments of the unfallen world. The beneficent development shown to be proceeding throughout the natural hierarchy is sharply contrasted with the perversions that result from changes in the course of the stars following human disobedience.

As was customary to the notion of natural causation, Milton particularly stresses the influence of the sun and stars on earthly development. His descriptions of solar and stellar influence, however, oppose the gentleness of their sway before the Fall to their postlapsarian asperity. Milton's unfallen sun neither transmits scorching heat nor enforces pinching cold, as it does after the Fall (10.691), but rather

> gently warms
> The Universe, and to each inward part
> With gentle penetration, though unseen,
> Shoots invisible virtue. . . .
>
> (3.583–86)

Blaming the Fall for the beginning of "influence malignant" and "Synod unbenign" among the stars (10.661–62), Milton shows them before the fall dispensing "soft fires" and "kindly heat," to "Temper or nourish, or in part shed down / Thir stellar virtue on all kinds that grow" (4.667–70).

This treatment of the influence of the celestial bodies turns the traditional theory of natural causation into a means of celebrating the dynamics of harmony in the unfallen world. The traditional notion that the sun prompts the development of minerals, for instance, informs not only the paean to its powers in Book 3 but also the imagery of gold and precious stones Milton uses in describing Eden. The "Sapphire Fount," with its "crisped Brooks, / Rolling on Orient Pearl and sands of Gold" (4.237–38), is borne on minerals that Milton suggests to have been tempered and glorified by the heat of "the Sun's more potent Ray" (4.673). Consequently, Milton's ideal landscape is not only "golden" in the traditional literary sense; it is also actively gilded by solar influence, indicating the dynamic processes of harmony and refinement with which Milton invests his unfallen world.

Sun and stars were traditionally held to govern animate as well as inanimate phenomena, and Milton shows them further contributing to the dynamic harmony of nature in causing the generation of creatures from the elements. In his creation account, Raphael describes all of the animals as emerging from the earth through spontaneous generation, but he distinguishes between the "perfect forms" of sexually reproducing species and the insects and worms reproduced by the power of the sun. The origin of such creatures had been particularly troublesome to commentators on Genesis, and Luther and Calvin had judged that harmful species among nature's minims were among the products of the fall.[12] Milton, however, resolves the problem of when such creatures appeared by stressing the beneficent influence of the prelapsarian sun. He associates the insects with the work of the sun by observing that they wear "Liveries deckt of Summer's pride / With spots of Gold and Purple, azure and green" (7.478–79), and with their source in the earth by noticing the "sinuous trace" with which they "streak the ground" (7.481). Similarly, the serpent's eyes of "Carbuncle" and "burnisht Neck of verdant Gold" (9.500–501) display the tempering influence of solar power, which precludes insects and worms from becoming harmful before the fall.

The trees and flowers of Milton's prelapsarian nature also grow continuously more pliant because they are tempered by the kindly sway of the celestial bodies. That fruit is "burnisht with golden rind," that herbs are "tender," that the rose is thornless (4.249–56)—all show the harmonious dynamics of natural causation and the temperateness of celestial influence, excluding from unfallen nature the growth of poisonous or thorny plants. Milton thus creates a network of pointed contrasts between the influences that work to develop harmony in the state of innocence and the perverse powers that impede and impair growth after human disobedience.

Milton's treatment of nature before the Fall, then, combines the stress on active agents of causation developed in Aristotelian and Thomistic thought with the notion of a prelapsarian state of harmony throughout nature advanced in Protestant commentaries on Genesis. This blend makes the harmony of nature in Milton's portrayal appear as a continuous, dynamic process of influence and response, extending throughout the created world. Such a vision provides two perspectives on Adam and Eve. First, as subjects of the influence of the stars, they are blessed by the gentleness of the larger powers that govern earthly development. Thus, they enjoy the "selectest influence," which the constellations cast on their nuptial bower to assure that their future offspring will be numerous and fortunate. From a second perspective, Adam and Eve are also participants in the dynamics of natural harmony. The parallel between the biological functions of male and female and the relationship of stars and earth established by the hierarchy of causes enables Milton to apply the same patterns and processes to both sets of relationships, magnifying Adam and Eve by their association with governing and subordinate elements of the larger world. Milton designs the relationship between Adam and Eve, like the relationship between the stars and the earth, to suggest a prospect of progressive, harmonious development.

Yet Milton's synthesis of the concept of natural causation with a Protestant view of the unfallen world also entails a second, more profound alteration of the Thomistic relationships among governing and governed parts of the hierarchy of causes. Instead of distinguishing sharply between positions of sway and positions of subjection in nature, Milton reshapes the hierarchical structure inherent in the theory of natural causation to suggest that man, together with all parts of the natural world, exists in a system of interdependent connections. Instead of showing subjects in the hierarchy of causes who simply receive the influence exerted upon them, Milton presents subjects who actively respond and, in responding, become in turn influences that promote development among superior members of the hierarchy. Such a reciprocity of sway and subjection, giving and receiving, makes Milton's use of the hierarchy of causes considerably different from that of Aquinas, for it implies that superior members are not simply governing agents but are at the same time affected by and dependent on those they govern. By postulating a world in which generative influence not only descends from active agents to their subjects, but responsively reascends from subjects to superiors, Milton converts the traditional hierarchy of causation into an interdependent system of interacting influences. He thereby creates a world susceptible to pollution on account of original sin, just as it is capable of progressive development as long as human integrity endures. For Milton treats nature as a system of relationships in which all parts are bound together by mutual influence, mutual action and mutual response.

Such chains of responsive influence stretch throughout Milton's treatment of subjects in the hierarchy of causes, beginning with his portrayal of the relationship between Adam and Eve. Milton shows Eve actively influencing Adam in a series of images that give her the powers of stimulating response elsewhere allocated to the sun and stars. Waking Eve, Adam beheld "Beauty, which whether waking or asleep, / Shot forth peculiar graces" (5.14–15). Like the sun that "Shoots invisible virtue even to the deep" (3.586), Eve "shot Darts of desire / Into all Eyes" (8.62–63). As the stars "shed down / Thir stellar virtue" (4.670–71), so Adam observes that a "thousand decencies . . . daily flow / From all her words and actions" (8.601–2). Pleading against Eve's proposal that they divide their labors, Adam argues, "I from the influence of thy looks receive / Access in every Virtue" (9.309–10). The influence that Milton shows Eve thus exerting to sweeten and strengthen Adam's growth confers upon woman a power of action and an importance that far exceed the restricted role Aquinas had allocated to females in the hierarchy of causes.

As responsive influence flows from Eve to Adam, so all earthly things react to the actions of generative agents by exerting responsive powers. "Mists and Exhalations" rise "from Hill or steaming Lake" (5.185–86), providing the "alimental recompense" that Raphael insists is necessary to sustain and feed even the stars and sun (5.4.24). In addition to exhaling such nutriments, the earth also emits light, having its own capacity to shine. Standing on the sun, Uriel points out the light of the earth (3.723); the epic narrator describes Raphael's view of the earth from the gates of heaven, where it appears "not unconform to other shining Globes" (5.259); and Raphael speculates that the light of the earth may be "as a Star" to the moon, shedding reciprocal influence (8.142).

Such reciprocity between governing agents and their subjects substantially modifies Thomistic notions of the relationship between the earth as subject and the stars as generative agents. Accepting a traditionally geocentric cosmos, Aquinas had treated the celestial bodies as independent causes, governing but not affected by anything on earth. Though Svendsen insists that Milton chose to retain the geocentric cosmos in *Paradise Lost*,[13] this view merits reconsideration. The epic narrator does not specifically describe astronomical relationships but shows innumerable stars and worlds within worlds (5.268). He makes Satan's route to the sun "up or down / By centre, or eccentric, hard to tell, / Or Longitude" (3.574–76). The theory of geocentricity is advanced primarily by Adam in his lectures to Eve, by Adam and Eve in their morning prayer, and by Adam again in his dialogue with Raphael. Though Raphael, relying on the anthropocentric language of Genesis, centers his creation account on the earth, his response to Adam's questions about astronomy presses the view advanced by the angelic chorus, which he has described in his account of the seventh day of creation. "Praising this new-made world" (7.617), the angels celebrate its

> Stars
> Numerous, and every Star perhaps a World
> Of destin'd habitation. . . .
> . . . among these the seat of men,
> Earth with her nether Ocean circumfus'd.
>
> (7.620–24)

In making the earth one star among stars numerous, Milton departs not only from the traditional geocentric cosmos, but also from the conception of causation that it supported. His departure serves to stress the reciprocity of influence between sun, stars, and earth, between giving and receiving in the hierarchy of causes.

Milton's modifications of these Thomistic notions serve to adapt the notion of natural causation to the Protestant view of Eden as a paradise within an unfallen world. Rather than setting Eden apart from the larger earth by exempting it from adversities outside of its boundaries, Milton, like Luther and

Calvin, presents an earthly paradise existing in a golden age. His treatment of the ideal landscape is not restricted to Eden, but extends to the larger domain of nature, whose prelapsarian harmony makes possible the happiness of the garden. Accordingly, Milton makes Eden not an exclusively human home, nor an ideal enclosure that circumscribes man's proper place in the natural order, but rather a center from which an expanding human population will extend to fill the earth. Adam, Raphael, Michael, and the angelic chorus of Book 7 know that the earth has been appointed, even before the Fall, as "the seat of men . . . / Thir pleasant dwelling place" (7.623, 625).

Their knowledge reconfirms Milton's insistence upon the interdependence of man and nature before the Fall—the dependence of human happiness on nature's harmony and the dependence of nature's harmony on human integrity. Rather than being banished from a protected place into a harsher domain, Milton's Adam and Eve, like Luther's and Calvin's, undergo a temporal exile from the concord of nature as a whole before the Fall into the discord of a world that has been subjected to a curse for their sake. In espousing the idea that nature as well as man was impaired by the Fall, Milton eschews not only St. Thomas's insistence on the constancy of processes of causation in the natural world, but also his vision of the state of innocence as an exclusively human optimum. Instead, Milton envisions in the earthly paradise a dynamic harmony that encompasses all parts of nature and that embraces man and nature, male and female, earth and the heavens in an interdependent, interacting order. Yet if Milton goes beyond the schoolman in idealizing the unfallen world, still, the dynamic processes and structured relationships he envisions in the state of innocence suggest that the poetry of his portrayal of paradise owes something to the patterns of thought advanced by the "lesser" teacher.

# Notes

1. Joseph E. Duncan, *Milton's Earthly Paradise: A Historical Study of Eden* (Minneapolis: University of Minnesota Press, 1972), pp. 70–74.

2. *Summa Theologica*, Pt. I, Q. 102, Art. 2; Pt. I, Q. 97, Art. 4; Pt. I, Q. 98, Arts. 1, 2; Pt. I, Q. 92, Art. 1, trans. Fathers of the English Dominican Province, 2d ed. (London: Burns Oates and Washbourne Ltd., 1922), 4:369; 341–3; 344–49; 274–76. Subsequent citations from the *Summa Theologica* also refer to the Dominican translation, 22 vols. (London: Burns Oates and Washbourne Ltd., 1915–27).

3. *Summa Theologica*, Pt. I, Q. 115 (London: Burns Oates and Washbourne Ltd., 1922), 150–67.

4. Ibid., Pt. I, Q. 102, Art. 2, 4:367–69.

5. Ibid., Pt. II-II, Q. 164, Art. 2 (London: Burns, Oates and Washbourne Ltd., 1921), 13:270–71.

6. Martin Luther, *Lectures on Genesis, Chapters 1–5*, trans. George V. Schick, *Luther's Works*, ed. Jaroslav Pelikan (St. Louis: Concordia Publishing House, 1958), 1:203–4; John Calvin, *A Commentarie of John Calvine, upon the first booke of Moses called "Genesis,"* trans. Thomas Tymme (London, 1578), pp. 110–11.

7. Both Luther and Calvin comment extensively on the evils superadded to the original design of nature because of original sin. Luther, for instance, observes that

the earth itself feels its curse. In the first place, it does not bring forth the good things it would have produced if man had not fallen. In the second place, it produces many harmful plants, which it would not have produced, such as darnel, wild oats, weeds, nettles, thorns, thistles. Add to these the poisons, the injurious venom, and whatever else there is of this kind.

See *Lectures on Genesis*, 1:204. Calvin similarly holds that "what corrupt thinges soever do growe, let us knowe that they are not the natural fruites of the earth, but corruptions which have their originall in sinne" and that "the intemperature of the aire, ice, thunders, unseasonable raines, drouthe, hailes and what soever is extraordinarie in the worlde, are the fruits of sinne." *A Commentarie*, pp. 112, 114.

8. Luther believes, for instance, that "before sin the air was purer and more healthful, and the water more prolific; yes, even the sun's light was more beautiful and clearer. Now the entire creation in all of its parts reminds us of the curse that was inflicted because of sin. *Lectures on Genesis*, 1:204.

Calvin comments on the unfallen world that "if so be the earth had not beene accursed for the sinne of man, all and everie parte thereof, as it was blessed from the beginning, should have beene the moste beautiful spectacle bothe of plentie, and also of pleasauntnesse; to be shorte, it had not ben unlik to Paradise, in comparison of the deformitie which we now behold." *A Commentarie*, p. 59.

9. So, for instance, Calvin observes that "there was no angle or corner of the earth which was at that time barren, nay there was none, but the same was verie rich & fruitful: but the blessing of God which in some other places was but meane, wonderfully had poured out it selfe in this place. Neither was there plentie onely for meate, but there was added also a great & delicate sweetenes for the taste of the mouth, & delectable comlines to the eye," describing Eden as the choicest spot in a pervasively paradisal world. *A Commentarie*, p. 61.

10. John Milton, *Paradise Lost, Complete Poems and Major Prose*, ed. Merritt Y.

Hughes (New York: The Odyssey Press, 1957). Subsequent citations of *Paradise Lost* are from this edition.

11. Kester Svendsen, *Milton and Science* (Cambridge, Mass.: Harvard University Press, 1956).

12. Luther observes that, before the Fall, "there were neither thorns nor thistles, neither serpents nor toads; and if there were any, they were neither venomous nor vicious." *Lectures on Genesis*, 1:77. Calvin excludes from the original work of creation "fleaze, lice, frogges, caterpillers, grassehoppers, and suche like hurtefull thinges." *A Commentarie*, pp. 52–53.

13. Svendsen, Milton and Science, pp. 48, 84–85.

# PART III
# *The Historical Dimension*

# Looking Back without Anger: Milton's Of Education

William Melczer

TWO preliminary remarks will help us on our way. First, Milton's concern with education surpasses the limits of this brief tractate we are examining here, the informal, eight-page pamphlet issued without title page, date, or publisher's name in 1644, and known as *Of Education*.[1] Such a necessary limitation, however, should by no means lead us to ignore Milton's wider concerns with the subject. Book 2 of the *De Doctrina Christiana*, or the famous passage from *Paradise Regained*,

> However many books
> Wise men have said are wearisom; who reads
> Incessantly, and to his reading brings not
> A spirit and judgment equal or superior,
> (And what he brings, what needs he elsewhere seek)
> Uncertain and unsettl'd still remains,
> Deep verst in books and shallow in himself,
> Crude or intoxicate, collecting toys,
> And trifles for choice matters, worth a spunge;
> As Children gathering pibles on the shore,[2]

should be a reminder for us that such and similar pronouncements of Milton ought eventually to be integrated into, and correlated with, our present findings concerning the tractate.

Second, brief as the pamphlet is, *Of Education* constitutes a considerably dense piece of writing, even by Miltonic standards, a piece of writing that may be examined from a number of different angles and from various points of view, depending upon what one is looking for. The concern here will be with but one single aspect of the work: Milton's relationship to the Middle Ages.

Even if one looks only for English works on the subject, Milton's *Of Education* does not appear as an isolated phenomenon. His tractate can be inserted within a string of works, some earlier, some written during the same period, but all growing out of a general awareness of continental humanistic education, with the later ones also being affected by early seventeenth-century naturalism, for example, through Francis Bacon's *Novum Organum.*[3] That string of works is very long. It is enough here to cite a few titles that are particularly relevant to Milton's tractate: Roger Ascham's *The Scholemaster;*[4] Richard Mulcaster's *Positions . . . necessary for the training up of children, either for skill in their books or health in their body;*[5] Humphrey Gilbert's *Queene Elizabethes Achademy;*[6] Henry Peacham's *The Compleat Gentleman;*[7] Henry Wotton's *Surveigh of Education;*[8] Samuel Hartlib's *A Reformation of Schooles;*[9] and many others. Hartlib's work is of particular interest for us, as it must have been for Milton, for Hartlib's own writings included English versions of a number of shorter works of the great Moravian theologian and educator, John Amos Comenius,[10] in particular of the *Praeludia*, the *Dilucidatio*, a table of "The Severall Titles of the Seven Parts of the Temple of Christian Pansophie," as well as chapter titles of the *Didactica Magna*, Comenius's masterpiece, written earlier, but published only later.[11] Milton knew, or at least he must have been aware, of all this.

What is Milton really proposing? A lengthy and tough curriculum of seven to eight years in which Latin, Greek, He-

brew, and Italian join forces to turn the "young un-
matriculated novices"[12] into educated gentry for whom (and,
on balance, only for whom) the whole curriculum was intended. Milton's ambitious *philological* program, probably
second to none among humanist educators, is so impressive
that this aspect of the curriculum stole the limelight of the
whole show. Since, as many critics have thought, [13] he outdid
all the other humanists in this respect, his must be the most
humanistic curriculum of all. Is this really so?

Milton's curriculum comprises grammar, arithmetic,
geometry, the Scriptures, agriculture, geography, navigation,
anatomy, physics, economics, politics, theology, Church history, Greek tragedy, Italian, poetry, and logic—in that order.
A closer look at the program reveals however that (1) the
trivium is split, appearing at the beginning and at the end of
the series; (2) an imperfect quadrivium is considerably expanded (with music occupying only a minor position); (3) at
the same time, the humanistic, that is to say, the man-
oriented subjects, lose their primacy to applied sciences such
as agriculture, geography, natural philosophy, navigation, et
cetera, all entailing a practice-oriented observation of nature;
(4) characteristically enough, the Scriptures, Church history,
and "apostolic scriptures," that is to say, the Fathers of the
Church, receive a renewed attention; and (5) though bodily
exercises are stressed, many of them are combined with war-
like endeavors, weapons, "military motions," of soldiership
on foot or on horseback.

The curricular analysis thus yields mixed results: the traditional humanistic emphasis on "anthropocentric subjects," as
Alberti would have called them,[14] is not really there, except
for the languages in which, however, form-drilling is bal-
anced with contents-saturation beyond the point Petrarch
would have liked to see it.[15] May we speak thus of Milton's
nonhumanistic perception of language? Hardly; though we
may indeed speak of a more pragmatic humanistic orienta-

tion, one in which the quasi-mystic aureole of the language tends to dissolve. Such an orientation comes obviously to the fore in Milton's theory of instrumentality.

"Language is but the *instrument* [italics added] conveying to us things useful to be known,"[16] he tells us. It is not an isolated case. Elsewhere he speaks of "what Religious, what glorious and magnificent *use* [italics added] might be made of Poetry."[17] Instrumentality becomes thus the handmaid of pragmatism. It is to convey the "solid things,"[18] "words and lexicons,"[19] "the substance of good things,"[20] (and not "meere words"[21]), and the "reall tincture of naturall knowledge"[22] that language is here to serve us. We are a far cry from Lorenzo Valla's exaltation of *eloquentia* for its own sake. Milton seems at this point to evidence a distinct Baconian naturalistic bent: more of a utilitarian approach than what we are usually willing to acknowledge.

To turn to a different area, the increasing confidence in direct observation and the necessary interaction between that observation and some of the mathematical sciences—present already in many fifteenth-century continental perceptions—become further accentuated in Milton's tractate. At the same time, though scholasticism is out of fashion, Aristotelianism is in vogue—a necessary post-Tridentine realization on both sides of the religious barricade. Modified forms of the trivium and the quadrivium continue to serve as the backbone of the program of studies. More important, the theological concerns, banned from the Arcadia of Italian humanistic education, are back in the fold once again. It is true that Milton is speaking in terms of a militant Puritan. But the necessary correlation in this case is not so much with English puritanism as it is with the spirituality of the Reform movement as a whole. That is the reason that the same theological concerns are back, much earlier than Milton, with Johann Sturm, the great educator of the Gymnasium in Strassbourg,[23] whose thought we find in England through his dense correspondence on matters humanistic with Roger Ascham; perhaps even more to the point, those same concerns are back with the aforementioned Johan Amos Comenius, whom Hartlib had personally known, and who had been in England himself just around the years of the publication of Milton's tract.[24]

In this regard, the idea of at least *some* ideological kinship with Comenius (mainly in the area of methodology) invites itself. Three concrete points of contact seem to be particularly relevant here:

1. Milton's pamphlet appeared two years after Hartlib's translation of one of Comenius's own treatises;
2. Milton refers to and quotes another work of Comenius, the *Januas*,[25] the "doorways" to language study;
3. Comenius's longer and more ambitious work, *Pansophia*, at least in its encompassing purpose, makes its presence felt on the pages *Of Education*.

The military concerns have been mentioned already. The preoccupation with physical fitness, present all along in the great Italian educational treatises, reemerges here, but clad in strongly suggestive medieval martial armor. This is also evident from an examination of Milton's definition of the more immediate civic objectives of education: "I call therefore a compleate and generous Education that which fits a man to perform justly, skilfully and magnanimously all the offices both private and publike of peace and war."[26] The passage recalls, of course, Aristotle in the *Politics*,[27] as well as Plato,[28] and even Quintillian's opening statement in the *Institutio Oratoria*. At the same time, however, it seems impossible to ignore the militant flavor of Milton's formulation, and it is hard to think that such an impression could have been unintentionally conveyed. In fact, the *militant*, and even the *military* aspect of the education imparted to the pupils, which we have considered earlier, goes hand in hand with the just reviewed appositely chosen definition, both of which are estranged bedfellows in Renaissance humanistic education, but which are, at the same time, precisely familiar bedfellows on the vaster medieval scene. It is with this vaster medieval scene that Milton's concept of the "reforming of education" (and that of others too, e.g., John Hall)[29] finds a natural kinship. For Hall as well as for Milton, the "reforming of education" was to be the last step in the militant Protestant Reformation.

A reconsideration of Aristotle has already been touched upon. But a reinterpreted Aristotelianism not only helped to differentiate between scholasticism and the more progressive Aristotelian modes of knowledge: it had another important side effect in the reconsideration and perhaps even reevaluation of the Middle Ages and a concomitant demystification of the Renaissance, or rather of the orthodox latinate humanism of the Renaissance.[30] Milton too was caught in the whirlwind of those upon whom it was beginning to dawn that the Petrarchan myth of the *re-naissance* was precisely that—a myth. The necessary ideological consequences of such a perception did not tarry to appear. They are also easy to follow. The period of the Middle Ages is not really what Renaissance self-infatuation thought it to be. Hence, there was a viable avenue to pursue: while rejecting arid scholasticism (that is to say, what was considered as such), it was possible to salvage, and to reconsider, other aspects of medieval thought. Spirituality was one: we remember Luther's own strong-willed perception in this regard; he felt himself to be the true spiritual heir to St. Augustine and St. Bernard.[31] In this regard, all told, we cannot simply forget that the Aristotelian "Felix qui potuit rerum cognoscere causam" becomes for Milton a Christian pietistic formulation: "The end then of learning is to repair the ruins of our first parents by regaining to know God aright, and out of that knowledge to love him, to imitate him, to be like him, as we may the neerest by possessing our souls of true vertue, which being united to the heavenly grace of faith makes up the highest perfection,"[32] a formulation akin to so many similar pronouncements that call to life a well-known Neoplatonic substratum in Marsilio Ficino, Leo Hebraeus, and others: knowledge is the condition for love.[33]

But, if we look carefully enough into the tractate, the return to Aristotelianism will appear manifest on deeper levels too: Milton's tendency to perceive things in universal, finite, well-defined, encompassing terms surfaces at various points: the act of composition is "organic,"[34] with exactingly "fitted stile";[35] literary genres (such as the epic) have "laws";[36] "decorum is . . . the grand master peece to observe";[37] pupils must be brought to the point of being "fraught with an universall insight into things";[38] learning must proceed in a "methodicall course";[39] the learning of "principles" is paramount.[40]

It is thus in a roundabout way that Milton outflanks the form-consciousness of Renaissance humanism in order to reestablish once again the preeminence of the substantive use of the concept. But it is precisely such conceptualized substance-orientation that constitutes one of the most prominent distinguishing features of the Aristotelianism and of the Aristotelian categorization of the Late Middle Ages.

Now, when we speak of Milton and the Middle Ages we must consider with the greatest care the cultural-philosophic momentum and *locus wherefrom* the great seventeenth-century master turns to us, and the historical categories that at that point are already left behind him and are, so to speak, history for him. In particular, we must not forget even for an instant that to speak of Milton and the Middle Ages is not the same as to speak of Petrarch and the Middle Ages, or even of Vittorino da Feltre, or Guarino da Verona, or Baldassare Castiglione and the Middle Ages—in order to remain within the boundaries of our subject on education.[41] While for Petrarch, the civic humanists (and Vittorino da Feltre and Guarino da Verona must be considered such), and the Neoplatonic humanists the Middle Ages—or better, that particular portion of the Middle Ages that elicited their own negative reaction, thirteenth-century Gothic scholasticism—constituted the *immediately preceding* vast cultural component against which they *rebelled* and used as an antitype to formulate their own alternative cultural programs, for the generation of Milton those same Middle Ages were not merely further removed in time but, more important, did not constitute anymore an unmediated previous cultural-philosophic realm, the reaction against which would have been an almost existential necessity. Instead, from Milton's vantage point, the background against which he was to assert himself was less monolithic and more variegated. The specific weight of its components proved far from uniform. What were these components? On the one hand, the still-lingering medieval scholasticism; on the other, the increasingly preoccupying trends of Renaissance humanism proper, in particular, of Italian Renaissance humanism. We shall now take these two categories, always within the circumscribed scope of our objective, one by one.

Medieval scholasticism and more particularly Aristotelian categorization had not exhausted themselves. In spite of the massive humanistic onslaught (mainly on the part of the ultra-orthodox Petrarchists and Neoplatonists)—or perhaps because of it—Aristotelianism in general and Aristotelian categorization in particular were alive and kicking. They were alive and kicking also as a consequence of the new Tridentine ideological consolidation that retreated inside the palisades of a safely guarded Aristotelianism after realizing, first gradually and then suddenly, the disastrous consequences that were in store for them, consequences issuing from the Neoplatonic recategorization. Though the virulent sphere of action of such Aristotelianism was particularly noticeable in the universities (Padua, Paris), these were by no means the only strongholds this philosophy could claim.[42] Milton himself knew but too well some of the literary-critical ends of this Aristotelianism, so much so that when he comes to recommend to his pupils the appropriate theoreticians of the art of letters, Aristotle, Horace, and their modern Italian commentators reign supreme:

> but that sublime art which in *Aristoteles poetics*, in *Horace*, and the *Italian* commentaries of *Castelvetro, Tasso, Mazzoni*, and others, teaches what the laws are of a true *Epic* poem, what of a *Dramatic*, what of a *Lyric*, what decorum is, which is the grand master peece to observe.[43]

Who are these Italian clients of Milton, these newborn reincarnations of the great Arab commentators that make of *Law* and *Decorum* (almost *law* and *order*) their new idol? Ludovico Castelvetro became famous as a result of his translation of Aristotle's *Poetics*;[44] Tasso's *Gerusalemme liberata*[45] and then (alas!) the *Gerusalemme conquistata*, of course loom large in the background of Milton's own epic poems. But Milton cites him here particularly because of his strongly Tridentine-flavored *Discorsi del poema eroico*.[46] Jacobi Mazzoni provided an Aristotelian defense of the *Divina Commedia*,[47] which had been not so much attacked by others as interpreted in less stringent Aristotelian terms. A reinterpreted Aristotelianism, steeped mainly in medieval rather than Renaissance tradition, appears thus firmly implanted in the background of Milton's mind no less than in his conceptions on education.

Even the perception that at least Milton's *methodological* bent is oriented toward the recently won didactic gains of the Renaissance remains not unassailable; it gives us a start to realize that Milton concludes his treatise with a hardly promising statement on the rough course of his proclaimed methodology: "This is not a bow for every man to shoot in that counts himself a teacher; but will require sinews almost equall to those which Homer gave Ulysses."[48] With the sinews Homer gave Ulysses, we are in a world of tough political commitments. Where now is Castiglione's *"sprezzatura"*?[49]

In conclusion, Milton's turning away from the Renaissance and embracing some of the tenets of the Middle Ages does not occur either unconditionally, or unequivocally. Quite to the contrary, the novel ideological reorientation is fraught with hesitations, at times with double allegiance, and more often than not with a sense of dichotomy whose formal elements gravitate toward the Renaissance, but whose substantive, content-charged elements hark back to the Middle Ages. One of the most eminent sons of the great spiritual revival unleashed by the Reformation, Milton, like so many of his earlier colleagues on the continent (recall d'Aubigné),[50] could not be so blind to the great form-culture issuing from the vastest classicizing movement since antiquity. But the demands of a post-Tridentine ideology in reform-Puritan garb impelled Milton toward tougher and more rigorously unitarian, in fact Aristotelian, positions whose main tenets were high standards of personal morality and Christian piety, and whose parallels, approximations, and time prototypes he could not have found in the Renaissance but could find farther back in the Middle Ages. In a way, *mutatis mutandis,* what we observe in *Of Education* is nothing but a rehearsal of what will happen later on an immensely larger scale of grandeur in the epic poems: Tasso's advice is heeded in formal, though not in substantive matters. All told, Milton could not have escaped the dictates of an ideology that he himself did so much to formulate.

## Notes

1. The following critical literature has been helpful: R. Quintana, "Note on English Educational Opinion during the Seventeenth Century," *SP* 27 (1930): 265–92; Herbert Kreter, *Bildungs- und Erziehungsideale bei Milton* (Halle: M.

Niemeyer, 1938); T. Hillway, "Milton's Theory of Education," *College English* 5 (1943–44): 376–79; M. G. Mason, "The Tractate of Education by John Milton, 1644," *Education* 74 (1953–54): 213–24; C. I. Smoth, "Some Ideas on Education before Locke," *Journal of the History of Ideas* 23 (1962): 403–6; W. R. Parker, "Education: Milton's Ideas and Ours," *College English* 24 (1962–63): 1–14; and J. F. Huntley, "*Proairesis, Synteresis,* and the Ethical Orientation of Milton's *Of Education,*" *PQ* 43(1964): 40–46. See also M. G. Parks, "Milton and Seventeenth-Century Attitudes on Education," Diss., University of Toronto, 1963.

2. *Paradise Regained,* 4.321–30. I have used the edition by John T. Shawcross, *The Complete English Poetry of John Milton* (New York: New York University Press, 1963).

3. 1620–23.

4. 1570.

5. 1581.

6. 1572.

7. 1622.

8. Before 1624(?).

9. 1642.

10. Or Jan Amos Kemonsky, 1592–1670. See Anna Heyberger, *Johan Amos Comenius: Sa Vie et son oeuvre d'éducateur* (Paris: H. Champion, 1928.).

11. Hartlib's publications of Comenius started in 1637.

12. *Complete Prose Works of John Milton,* ed. Don M. Wolfe (New Haven, Conn.: Yale University Press, 1959), 2:374. The text of *Of Education* is on 2:362–415. This is the edition to which I refer in the present study.

13. See n. 1 above.

14. Cf. Giuseppe Saitta, *L'educazione dell'umanesimo in Italia* (Venice: "La Nuova Italia," 1928), passim.

15. Concerning the immense bibliography on Petrarch, see, in particular, Ernst Cassirer, *Individuum und Kosmos in der Philosophie der Renaissance* (Leipzig and Berlin: B. G. Teubner, 1927).

16. P. 369.

17. Pp. 405–6.

18. P. 369.

19. Ibid.

20. P. 374.

21. P. 376.

22. P. 394.

23. On Sturm, see my own "La Pensée éducative de Jean Sturm dans les *Classicae epistolae*" (Montpellier: Centre d'Histoire de la Réforme et du Protestantisme de l'Université Paul Valéry, 1973), pp. 125–41.

24. Cf. George Henry Turnbull, *Hartlib, Dury and Comenius* (Liverpool: University Press of Liverpool, 1947).

25. Actually, *Janua linguarum reserata.*

26. Pp. 377–79.

27. VII. viii.

28. *Laws* 1.643.

29. *The Advancement of Learning,* 1649.

30. Still fundamental is Pierre De Nolhac, *Pétrarque et l'humanisme* (Paris: Champion, 1907).

31. See my own "The Winged Vessel," Diss., University of Iowa, 1969.

32. Pp. 366–67.

33. On Ficino, see Paul Oskar Kristeller, *The Philosophy of Marsilio Ficino* (New York: Columbia University Press, 1943); on Leo Hebraeus, H. Pflaum, *Die Idee der Liebe: Leone Ebreo* (Tübingen: J. C. B. Mohr, 1926), and the present writer's "Platonisme et Aristotélisme dans la pensée de Léon l'Hébreu," in *Platon et Aristote à la Renaissance* (Tours: Centre d'Études Supérieures de la Renaissance, 1973), pp. 293–306.

34. P. 401.

35. Ibid.

36. P. 405.

37. Ibid.

38. P. 406.

39. Ibid.

40. P. 414. This by inference only.

41. Paul Oskar Kristeller's perceptions are, in this regard, fundamental: *Studies in Renaissance Thought and Letters* (Rome: Storia e letteratura, 1956), and *Renaissance Thought: The Classic, Scholastic, and Humanistic Strains* (New York: Harper, 1961), among others.

42. Cf. Eugenio Garin, *La filosofia* (Milan: Vallarchi, 1947); and Giovanni Gentile, *Il pensiero italiano del Rinascimento* (Florence: G. C. Sansoni, 1940).

43. Pp. 404–5.

44. 1570.

45. 1580/81.

46. 1587.

47. 1573–87.

48. P.415.

49. *Il cortigiano*, 1525, but written much earlier. The term is quite untranslatable: a nonchalant, graceful way of being and of behaving.

50. See n. 31 above.

# [ 6 ]
# *Milton among the Monks*
## Michael Lieb

IN the history of clerical satire, few institutions have suffered greater castigation than monasticism. This venerable calling, known for its piety and devotion and for its promulgation of culture, became the butt of the satirist's gibes throughout the Middle Ages and the Renaissance. Those critical of the calling saw it as a source of corruption in religious as well as secular affairs. One need only be reminded of Chaucer's Monk to recognize the prevailing attitude. Hardly one devoted to the vows of poverty, chastity and obedience, this "fair prelaat" is "An outridere, that lovede venerie." Caring not a jot for "The reule of seint Maure or of seint Benoit," "This ilke Monk leet olde thynges pace, / And heeld after the newe world the space."[1] If Chaucer's Monk is typical of the antimonastical outlook that emerged in the Middle Ages, that outlook found expression time and again in the centuries that followed. One of the most able Renaissance spokesmen was Erasmus, no stranger himself to the monastical calling. His work *The Praise of Folly* represents a fitting example of the contempt in which monasticism was held on the eve of the Reformation. The very embodiments of "Vileness, Ignorance, Rudeness and Impudence," monks, we find, are detested by all men. Rather than being called Christians, "they call themselves Cordiliers, and among these too, some are Colletes, some Miners, some Minims, some Crossed; and agen, these are

Benedictines; these Carmelites, those Augustines; these Williamites, and those Jacobines. . . . And of these, a great part build so much on their Ceremonies and petty Traditions of Men, that they think one Heaven is too poor a reward for so great merit; little dreaming that the time will come when Christ, not regarding any of these trifles, will call 'em to account for His precept of Charity."[2] If the attitudes expressed here became widespread during the Reformation, they were legion in England. Anti-monastical sentiment manifested itself both in word and in deed, as those who suffered under Thomas Cromwell's dissolution of the monasteries during the reign of Henry VIII could attest. Monasticism fared no better in the following century, which brought to the fore once again anti-monastical attitudes that by then had had a long and venerable tradition.

It is within the context of this tradition, of course, that Milton's own views are to be seen.[3] As one who sought to carry on the work of the Reformation in the face of prelatical corruption, Milton was an inveterate despiser of monks. He saw them as none other than the forebears of the Anglican prelates that were destroying his country. Anglicanism, he argued, was merely an offshoot of Romanism; and Romanism, with its "easy Confession, easy Absolution, Pardons, Indulgences, Masses . . . , *Agnus Dei's,* Reliques, and the like," was the religion of the devil, founded upon the practices of monks (6. 179). Milton held this view to the end of his life. As such, his anti-monastical outlook is simply the product of what Don M. Wolfe has called "the limits of Miltonic toleration."[4] When it comes to monks, those limits are drawn tight indeed. Not that Milton despised all monks. On the contrary, he was a great admirer of figures like St. Basil the Great, one of the founders of monasticism.[5] But his admiration extended to their accomplishments, not to their calling. "[W]hat though *Luther* and other Monks" were "reformers"? he quips in *Animadversions;* "does it follow therefore that

Monks ought to continue?" (3. 178). As a child of the Reformation, Milton revealed an intolerance of anything that
smacked of Romanism. Judging by his treatment of monks
and monasticism throughout his career, this outlook is not at
all inconsistent with his practices as a writer. An exploration
of that outlook and its impact upon his writings should provide insight not only into his religious views but into his
prevailing habits of mind.

Milton's distaste for monasticism appears as early as his
prolusions. There he expresses his contempt for scholastic
philosophy as the "joyous wranglings of crabbed old men,
which, born . . . in the cells of monks, are betrayed by their
odor and exhale the savage sterness of their authors and ex-
hibit the frowns of the fathers" (3. 161). The "blind Ignorance" of scholasticism, he says, arose in the Middle Ages
with "the absurd dogmas of most stupid monks" (3. 259).
Such stupidity, Milton later maintains in *The Reason of
Church-Government,* is reflected in the universities of his
own times, where students are "fed with nothing else but the
scragged and thorny lectures of monkish and miserable
sophistry" (3. 273). It was a point he was to make at length in
*Of Education.* Bad learning is not all that Milton associates
with monasticism, however. Idolatry and superstition for
Milton are also monkish attributes. On the first score, Milton
relates, in *Of Prelatical Episcopacy,* the way in which monks
would "patronize their Idolatry" whenever iconoclasts attempted to "abolish Images" (3. 100). On the second score,
Milton maintains in *The Second Defence* that monks "were
used to have recourse to all manner of spectres and imaginary
monsters" (8. 45). Added to this list of charges is that of
celibacy, a custom that Milton could not abide. In this sense,
the very meaning of the word *monk* as μοναχός or "solitary"
was suspect to him. Thus he refers in the preface to the *Judge-
ment of Martin Bucer* to the "canonicall tyranny of stupid and
malicious Monks," who, "in the worst and weakest ages of

knowledge," "having rashly vow'd themselves to a single life, which they could not undergoe, invented new fetters to throw on matrimony, that the world thereby waxing more dissolute, they also in a general loosnes might sin with more favor" (4. 9).

Monkish celibacy in the Middle Ages, then, becomes for Milton a prime cause in his own age of clerical restraints upon divorce. These restraints are of a kind, moreover, with that thwarting of natural desire which is the basis of a happy marital relationship and without which the marriage will prove to be unhealthy. It is precisely in celebration of this desire that Milton in *Paradise Lost* sings, "Hail wedded Love, mysterious Law, true sourse / Of human ofspring, sole pro- prietie, / In Paradise of all things common else" and castigates those "Hyppocrites" who "austerely talk / Of puritie and place and innocence, / Defaming as impure what God de- clares / Pure" (4: 744–52). "[W]ho bids abstain," Milton asks, "But our Destroyer, foe to God and Man?" (4. 748–749). Monkish celibacy, then, has no place in Milton's world. On a larger scale, it involves for Milton a denial of experience, a turning away from one's responsibility to choose between right and wrong as a result of being fully aware of both sides. This is the point that Milton makes in *Areopagitica*. It is in a sense monkish prohibitions that accordingly prompt him to declare, "I cannot praise a fugitive and cloister'd vertue unex- ercis'd & unbreath'd, that never sallies out and sees her adver- sary, but slinks out of the race, where that immortall garland is to be run for, not without dust and heat" (4. 311). Monks and the monastical point of view, therefore, do not fare very well in Milton's hands.

Nowhere does this fact emerge more clearly than in his *History of Britain*, which is as much a history of medieval monasticism as it is an account of the military, civil, and political life of England *"From the first traditional Beginning, continu'd to the Norman Conquest,"* to quote Milton's subti-

tle. In fact, the history itself was undertaken largely to correct, as much as possible, what Milton believed to be the
gross errors of his sources, many of them monks. Although
Milton closely follows such sources as Bede, he has nothing
but contempt for figures like Geoffrey of Monmouth. Milton's attitude toward Geoffrey, among other monkish
sources, may be seen in the statement that concludes the second book of his history. Having treated pre-Roman and Roman Britain in the first two books, Milton laments the demise
both of the Roman Empire and of the Roman influence itself:
"with the Empire fell also what before in this Western World
was cheifly *Roman;* Learning, Valour, Eloquence, History,
Civility, and eev'n Language it self, all these together, as it
were, with equal pace diminishing, and decaying." "Hence-
forth," he laments, "we are to stear by another sort of Authors; near anough to the things they write, as in thir own
Countrie, if that would serve; in time not much belated, some
of equal age; in expression barbarous . . . ; in civil matters . . .
dubious Relaters, and still to the best advantage of what they
term holy Church, meaning indeed themselves: in most matters of Religion, blind, astonish'd, and strook with superstition as with a Planet; in one word, Monks" (10. 101–2). The
statement triumphantly sums up Milton's attitude. It suggests
his contempt for monks not only as sources of historical information but also as purveyors of religious belief.

From the first point of view, they represent a prime cause
of Milton's abandonment of his plans to write an Arthuriad.
As we all know, Milton had projected such an enterprise as
early as *Mansus* and the *Epitaphium Damonis,* and had mentioned it again in the preface to the second book of *The
Reason of Church-Government.* His disenchantment with the
Arthurian material, recorded in *The History of Britain,* he
attributes to the unreliability of his monkish sources: "But
who *Arthur* was, and whether ever any such reign'd in *Britain,*" Milton says, "hath been doubted heertofore, and may

again with good reason. For the Monk of *Malmsbury,* and others whose credit hath sway'd most with the learneder sort, we may well perceave to have known no more of this *Arthur* 500 years past, nor of his doeings, then we now living; And what they had to say, transcrib'd out of *Nennius,* a very trivial writer ·yet extant. . . . Or out of a *British* Book, the same which he of *Monmouth* set forth, utterly unknown to the World, till more then 600 years after the dayes of *Arthur.* . . . Others of later time have sought to assert him by old legends and Cathedrall regests. But he who can accept of Legends for good story, may quickly swell a volume with trash, and had need be furnish'd with two only necessaries, leasure, and beleif, whether it be the writer, or he that shall read" (10. 127–28). Such an attitude, of course, accounts for Milton's castigation of "fabl'd Knights" with their "Races and Games" and "tilting Furniture, emblazon'd Shields, / Impreses quaint, Caparisons and Steeds," and the like, in *Paradise Lost* (9. 29–38). If the Arthur of Geoffrey and the other monks appears at all in Milton's epic, he is associated with none other than Satan and his crew, who are compared to "*Uthers* Son / Begirt with *British* and *Armoric* Knights" (1. 580–81). In Milton's denigration of the kind of legendary world that he found portrayed in his monastical sources and the romances to which they gave rise, we become aware of his insistence upon recounting history in its most reliable form. We become aware, that is, of his concern with the nature of truth as a historical fact. For the poet of *Paradise Lost,* this meant transcribing the truths of Christian history as he found them in the Bible. For the author of *The History of Britain,* this meant transcribing the truths of his nation's past as he found them in the most dependable records he could obtain. In both cases it meant dismissing anything that smacked of monastic duplicity.

This attitude accounts for much of the monastic satire that Milton incorporates into both his epic and his history. In his

epic we recall Satan's adventures in that limbo of winds later
known as the Paradise of Fools. Here, we learn, are
transported "Embryo's and Idiots, Eremites and Friers/
White, Black, and Grey, with all thir trumperie. / Here Pil-
grims roam . . . who to be sure of Paradise/ Dying put on the
weeds of *Dominic*, / Or in *Franciscan* think to pass disguis'd"
(3. 474–80). In their false pursuit of paradise, they fly up to
this place, "pass[ing] the Planets seven" and the "fixt" stars
until "Saint *Peter* at Heav'ns Wicket seems/ To wait them
with his Keys, and now at foot/ Of Heav'ns ascent they lift
thir Feet, when loe/ A violent cross wind from either Coast/
Blows them transverse ten thousand Leagues awry/ Into the
devious Air; then might ye see/ Cowls, Hoods and Habits
with thir wearers tost/ And fluttered into Raggs, then Reliques, Beads/ Indulgences, Dispenses, Pardons, Bulls, / The
sport of Winds: all these upwhirld aloft/ Fly o're the backside
of the World" (3. 481–94), lost in this afterlife of their own
delusions. The pattern of flight undermined by a sudden ig-
nominious drop recounted here is not unique to Milton's
monastic satire in *Paradise Lost*. It is dramatically anticipated
by an event that Milton obviously delights in recounting in
*The History of Britain*. There, he tells about "*Elmer* a Monk
of *Malmsbury*," who thought that he could prognosticate future events but "who could not foresee, when time was, the
breaking of his own Legs for soaring too high. He in his
youth strangely aspiring, had made and fitted Wings to his
Hands and Feet; with these on the top of a Tower, spread out
to gather air, he flew more then a Furlong; but the wind being
too high, came fluttering down to the maiming of all his
Limbs; yet so conceited of his Art, that he attributed the
cause of his fall to the want of a Tail, as Birds have, which he
forgot to make to his hinder parts" (10. 307–8). This incident,
as Milton narrates it, recapitulates his attitude toward monks
and all they signify: as symbols of false aspiration and pride,
they suffer the humiliation of those who attempt to create and

inhabit a world of illusion. Their fate is to be cut off in midflight and to suffer the ignominy of an unexpected and precipitous fall.

As Milton conceives them, however, monks represent the consummate expression not only of the self-deceived but of the deceiver who would foist his illusory world upon others. The idea returns us to Milton's reference in *Paradise Lost* to all those "Eremites" "disguis'd" in "Cowls, Hoods, and Habits." In this context one thinks both of the Comus of Milton's *Mask* and of the Satan of *Paradise Regained:* each is disguised as a hermit whose attire owes something to the monastical tradition.[6] For Milton, that tradition would have its most immediate antecedent in the Archimago of *The Faerie Queene.* There that arch-deceiver is disguised as a "holy father" "in long black weeds y-clad, / His feet all bare, his beard all hoary gray; / And by his belt his book he hanging had . . . / . . . [A]ll the way he prayed as he went, / And often knocked his breast as one that did repent."[7] Archimago certainly anticipates the arch-deceivers of Milton's epics, not to mention his masque. For this reason, Milton maintains in *The History of Britain* that, as a result of their duplicity, monks are none other than "Ministers of . . . the Devil" (10. 307).

In that capacity they become purveyors of false religious beliefs, leading to monastical corruption of the worst sort. For Milton, the introduction of such corruption onto English soil is attributable to none other than *"Austin,"* "the monk, who first brought" the *Romish* religion into *England* from *Gregory* the Pope" (6.66). Thus, in his *History* Milton relates the well-known story (found in Bede and elsewhere) of Gregory's association of the pagan *"Angli"* with "Angels" and of his consequent decision to convert the *"Angli"* to Christianity. Accordingly, Milton says, Gregory "sent *Augustine*" and "other zealous Monks" to "preach . . . the Gospel" to "the *English* Nation." In relating the account of Augustine's journey, Milton is at pains to emphasize the "carnal fear" that hampered his mission and his use of superstitious images in finally carrying out his mission. In fact, after Augustine gained a foothold, he surrounded himself, Milton implies, with all the vestiges of Romanism: "vessels and vestments for the Altar, Coaps, reliques, and . . . a Pall to say Mass in: to such a rank superstition that Age was grown." "*Austin* thus exalted to Archiepiscopal authority, recover'd from the ruins and other profane uses, a Christian Church in *Canterbury* built of old by the *Romans;* which he dedicated by the name of Christs Church, and joyning to it built a seat for himself and his successors; a Monastery also neer the Citty Eastward, where *Ethelbert* of his motion built St. *Peters,* and enrich't it with great endowments, to be a place of burial for the Archbishops and Kings of *Kent:* so quickly they step't up into fellowship of pomp with Kings" (10.143–46).

This account, in turn, is followed by one that is even more incriminating. It involves Augustine's attempt to subjugate other monks. Warned that they should follow Augustine only if they find him "meek and humble," they discover that he "[bears] himself proudly." In his meeting with them, he "neither arose to meet [them], nor receiv'd [them] in any brotherly sort, but sat all the while pontifically in his Chair." When they refuse to obey him, he replies, "since ye refuse to accept of peace with your brethren, ye shall have War from your enemies; and since ye will not with us preach the word of life, to whom ye ought, from their hands ye shall receive death." This, in turn, is followed eventually by a massacre of the monks who opposed Augustine. Although, Milton comments, Bede attempts to "excuse *Austin* of this bloodshed" by suggesting that Augustine was "dead long before" the actual massacre occurred, Augustine cannot be excused; by Milton's computations, he must still be alive (10:147–50).

Be that as it may, the entire incident had so great an impact upon Milton that he considered writing a drama based upon it. Thus, in the Cambridge Manuscript, we find, among his other outlines for tragedies inspired by the events of British history, his plan to write a drama on "the slaughter of the monks of Bangor by Edelfride stirrd up as is said by Ethelbert, and he by Austine the monke because the Britains would not receave the rites of the Roman Church" (18.242). This is only one among a number of projected dramas on the influence of monastic corruption.[8] If nothing else, it reveals Milton's interest in that subject not only for its historical value but for its possible literary significance. In fact, Milton's account of the monastical corruptions embodied in the figure of Augustine in *The History of Britain* reveals both a flair for the dramatic and a penchant for portraying scenes that suggest later poetic renderings. Augustine's "exaltation," his delight in idolatry, his building a "seat" for himself, his attempt to subjugate others, his arrogant posture of sitting "pontifically in his Chair," his recourse to vengeance: all these characteristics assume Satanic significance in *Paradise Lost*. All, in fact, are summed up in the well-known opening of the second book: "High on a Throne of Royal State, which far / Outshon the wealth of *Ormus* and of *Ind* . . . / Satan exalted sat, by merit rais'd / To that bad eminence" (2.1–6). On his own temple seat, Satan "aspires / Beyond thus high," as he devises ways of wreaking vengeance upon all who defy him (1.6–9). In that way he is the fitting symbol of all those evils which Milton portrayed in such monastical figures as Augustine of Kent in *The History of Britain*.

The corruptions that Augustine initiated, finally, assume more than local significance in Milton's account. For Milton, they are the very source of the religious, political, and social weaknesses that brought about the Norman conquest (10.316). As such, Milton maintains, these evils should serve as a warning to all those who might tend to overlook the effects of prelatical corruption in his own age. Thus Milton ends his history with a warning to his times that they "remember this Age" and "fear from like Vices without amendment the Revolution of like Calamities" (10.316). It was a point he put to polemical use time and again in his tracts against the clergy: true Reformation would come only when England was prepared to free itself of the trammels of its monastical past, to purify itself, he declares in *Of Reformation*, from the pollutions wrought by the "hands of *Bishops, Abbots,* and *Monks*" (3.46). *Paradise Lost* itself, we recall, culminates in a vision of ecclesiastical corruption, wherein "Wolves shall succeed for teachers, grievous Wolves" who "turn" "all the sacred mysteries of Heav'n" "to thir own vile advantages" "of lucre and ambition" and "taint" "the truth" "with superstitions and traditions" (12.508–12). "Truth" then "shall retire / Bestuck with slandrous darts," and "the World" shall "goe on, / To good malignant, to bad men benigne, / Under her own waight groaning" (12.535–39). Although the context here extends far beyond the monastical framework established by *The History of Britain,* the historical ties that Milton established throughout his career as polemist cannot be overlooked. The Reformation fervor that inspires his prose tracts and is, in fact, anticipated in such works as *Lycidas* assumes apocalyptic significance in *Paradise Lost,* as Milton awaits that "day" "of respiration to the just, / And vengeance to the wicked" when man's "saviour" and "Lord" will "be reveald" "from Heav'n" "In glory of the Father, to dissolve / *Satan* with his perverted World, then raise / From the conflagrant mass, purg'd and refin'd, / New Heav'ns, new Earth, Ages of endless date" (12.539–49). One may be assured that, as far as Milton is concerned, the perversions cleansed by this event will involve all those that he included under the title of monk.

## Notes

1. General Prologue in *The Canterbury Tales,* in *The Works of Geoffrey Chaucer,* ed. F. N. Robinson, 2d ed. (Boston: Houghton Mifflin, 1957), 11.165–207. Compare the description of the Friar in the General Prologue (11.208–69). After the Reformation, the offices of monk and friar were generally not distinguished.

2. Desiderius Erasmus, *The Praise of Folly*, trans. John Wilson (1668), in *Prose and Poetry of the Continental Renaissance*, ed. Harold H. Blanchard (New York and London: Longmans, Green, 1949), pp. 563–64.

3. All references in my text to Milton's prose are from *The Works of John Milton*, ed. Frank Allen Patterson, 18 vols. in 21 (New York: Columbia University Press, 1931–38). All references to Milton's poetry in my text are from *The Complete Poetry of John Milton*, ed. John T. Shawcross (Garden City, N.Y.: Doubleday and Co., 1971).

4. See Wolfe's article of that title in *Journal of English and Germanic Philology* 60 (1961): 834–46. Even when monasticism was not specifically a product of Romanism, Milton was unflinching in his castigation. See his treatment of monks in *A Brief History of Muscovia* (10:336–40). Milton would have blanched indeed had he known that one Edward Pettit was to associate him with monasticism in *The Vision of Purgatory* (London, 1680). There Milton is conceived as desiring entrance into the "Backgate" of a monastic purgatory. Entreating "a Provincial of the Jesuits" to aid his cause, Milton argues that he has "promot[ed]" Jesuitical "Interests," "attend[ed] their Consults, and observ[ed] their Orders" (pp. 98–100). I am indebted to Professor John T. Shawcross for this reference.

5. See comments on Basil in *Of Reformation* (3:32), *Apology* (3:286), *Tetrachordon* (4:211), *Tenure* (5:234), etc.

6. See *A Mask* (11.166–67; compare 11.390–92) and *Paradise Regained* (1.314–15).

7. Edmund Spenser, *Books I and II of The Faerie Queene*, ed. Robert Kellogg and Oliver Steele (New York: The Odyssey Press, 1965), I.i.29. See also Erasmus, *The Colloquies*, especially "The Well-to-do Beggars," trans. Craig R. Thompson (Chicago: University of Chicago Press, 1965).

8. For example, compare the following notations: "Edwin son to Edward the yonger for lust depriv'd of his kingdom or rather by faction of monks when he hated together the imposter Dunstan"; "Edward son of Edgar murderd by his step-mother to which may be inserted the tragedie stirred up betwixt the monks and preists about mariage" (18:241–44).

## [ 7 ]
# The Medieval View of Christian History in Paradise Lost

Albert C. Labriola

THE Low German Bible that Steffen Arndes printed at Lübeck in 1494 contains 152 illustrations. The one of Jacob dreaming (Gen. 28) shows him asleep while he sits on the ground with his back propped up against a tree. The bottom of a ladder on which angels are ascending rests against his torso, and God the Father appears in the heavens at the summit of the ladder. On the ground alongside Jacob is a rod or staff on which his left hand is resting. This illustration correlates three significant images in Christian iconography—the rod or staff, the ladder, and the tree.[1] In numerous variations the typological image of wood recurs throughout the Old Testament—in the ark that delivered Noah and his family from the Deluge, the lintels and doorposts marked with the blood of the Paschal lamb, the tree or bush from which God communicated to Moses, the rod by which Moses worked miracles and led the Israelites out of bondage, the staff on which the brazen serpent was uplifted, the pole on which the scouts carried the bunch of grapes from the Promised Land, the ladder seen by the sleeping Jacob, the crossed sticks in the hands of the Samaritan woman seen by Elijah, and the twigs carried by Isaac, who was to have been his father's sacrifice to the Lord. These images signify the self-revelation of God to His chosen people, the communication and interaction be-

115

tween God and man, and God's encouragement of mankind to be saved.

From a typological perspective these and similar variations of the image of wood acquire their greatest significance in relation to the events of the New Testament they prefigure. These images prefigure the use and function of the cross during the Paschal triduum, the three-day period of Christ's ministry from Good Friday to Easter Sunday, including His Passion and Death, the Harrowing of Hell, and the Resurrection. The cross becomes the central symbol of the so-called Paschal Mystery, of Christ's ministry of Redemption. At the beginning of the Paschal triduum, the cross is the means of humiliation and suffering; later it is the instrument of triumph and victory. In a similar way the suffering or patient Christ (*Christus Patiens*) becomes the conquering or triumphant Christ (*Christus Victor*).

Early in his career Milton envisioned a tragedy on the topic "*Christus Patiens.*" As the brief outline in the Trinity manuscript makes clear, the drama would have centered on the New Testament theme of the suffering of Christ and His patient endurance. The play was to have depicted the suffering in Gethsemane and the betrayal by Judas; finally, Christ's agony was to have received "noble expressions."[2] The topic "*Christus Patiens*" is followed by three others: "Christ Bound," "Christ Crucifi'd," and "Christ Risen." As sequential elements in the same work or as topics for separate dramas, such a listing indicates that dominant ideas in Milton's mind included Christ's humiliation and exaltation, Christ's heroic manifestation of patience, and the triumph that followed.

Although Milton did not write dramas on these topics, the themes were never far from his mind. They are, in fact, the major themes of much of his major poetry. Christ's manifestation of patience begins at the Incarnation and culminates with the activities of the Paschal triduum. For Milton,

Christ's patience was supremely exercised in the humiliation and suffering of the Passion and Death. As the Suffering Servant or *Ebed Yahweh,* Christ provides the pattern and norm for Christian heroism.[3] In the incomplete poem entitled "The Passion," which was to have celebrated some of the activities of the Paschal triduum, Milton calls Christ the "Most perfect Hero" (1.13).[4] In *Paradise Regained* Christ's exercise of patience in the Wilderness is preparatory to the supreme exercise later at the Passion and Death; and in *Paradise Lost* Adam, having learned from Michael about Christ's ministry of Redemption, asserts "that suffering for Truth's sake / Is fortitude to highest victory" (12.569–70). He also asserts that he has been "Taught" the heroism of patience by the "example" of the "Redeemer" (12.572–73). If patience and Christian heroism are stressed in Milton's poetry, they are likewise emphasized in his prose, especially in *De Doctrina Christiana*—where in the chapter on the ministry of Redemption he develops the view that patience and its reward are best reflected in the humiliation and exaltation of Christ, the pattern to which mankind should conform. To emphasize the paramount importance of mankind's participation in Christ's heroism, Milton cites a number of proof-texts, including Romans 8:17, 29; 2 Timothy 2:11–12; Ephesians 2:5–6; 1 Peter 4:13. These proof-texts, which allude to the Paschal Mystery and mankind's participation in it, emphasize that mankind must suffer with Christ in order to be exalted with Him.

Mankind's imitation of Christ, especially of the suffering Christ *(Christus Patiens),* is periodically stressed throughout *De Doctrina Christiana,* and many of the proof-texts cited in the previous paragraph, as well as others closely related, are employed again and again. There is no better example than Milton's discussion of the sacrament of Baptism. Milton repeatedly mentions that the sign or ceremony of Baptism, immersion in running water, is intended to "signify" *("significandam")* the believers' "regeneration by the Holy

Spirit, and their union with Christ in his death, burial, and resurrection" (16:168–69). Having cited some of St. Paul's comments on Baptism, including 1 Corinthians 12:13; Galatians 3:27; Romans 6:3; Colossians 2:12, Milton remarks that the sacrament "was intended to represent figuratively [*figurate . . . significat*] the painful life of Christ, his death and burial, in which he was immersed . . . for a season" (16:184–85). Referring again to St. Paul, Milton stresses the same points: "that baptism is not merely an initiatory rite, but a figurative representation of our death, burial, and resurrection with Christ" (16:190–91). Baptism thereby enables mankind to commemorate and participate in Christ's Paschal triumph.

In Milton's view the Paschal triumph, mankind's participation in it, and the sign or ceremony of the sacrament that celebrates it also recall certain Old Testament personages and events prefiguring both the Paschal triumph and the rite of Baptism. Citing Petrine and Pauline proof-texts (for instance, 1 Peter 3:20–21), Milton observes that "Noah's ark was the type of Baptism" and was "the like figure whereunto even baptism doth also now save us" (16:190–91). Echoing St. Paul (1 Cor. 10:2), Milton remarks that "all our fathers were baptized unto Moses in the cloud and in the sea" (16:190–91). In *Paradise Lost* Noah, Moses, and many other Old Testament personages are included among the "shadowy Types" (12.303) who prefigure Christ's ministry of Redemption. In Milton's thinking the Paschal triumph is central to an understanding of biblical history, typological correspondence, and sacramental celebration.

The principal events of the Paschal triduum—Christ's Suffering and Death, the Harrowing of Hell, and Resurrection—constitute a frame of reference in which much of the action and characterization of *Paradise Lost* may be interpreted. Using techniques of irony, inversion, and parody, Milton characterizes Satan as the demonic counterpart of *Christus*

*Patiens* and *Christus Victor.*[5] He highlights the "cunning resemblances" (to use a phrase from *Areopagitica*) between Satan's raising of the fallen angels from the burning lake and
Christ's achievement of the Paschal triumph. In raising the
fallen angels, Satan undertakes the demonic counterpart of
Christ's ministry of Redemption. In seeking to undergo the
cycle of humiliation and exaltation, he displays parodic or
"cunning resemblances" to Christ's heroism. From these
ironic comparisons, others follow. Satan's actions at the
burning lake are also compared to certain Old Testament
prefigurations of the Paschal triumph, including Noah,
Moses, and others, and to the mimetic and symbolical
reenactment of the Paschal triumph in the sacrament of Baptism. In the present essay I intend to suggest how and why
only one Old Testament prefiguration, Noah and the Deluge,
fits into the larger context I have described.

In *The Legend of Noah* Don Cameron Allen observes that
the account of Noah and the Deluge "was always considered
one of the best allegorical adumbrations of the life and ministry of Christ"; it was also traditionally interpreted as "the
story of the second creation and the first salvation."[6] As the
Redemption has been interpreted by the Church Fathers and
depicted in iconography, it too is an act of re-creation because
mankind, spiritually dead since the fall, is upraised and revived through the Paschal triumph of Christ. In the art of the
catacombs, Christ sometimes resembles Noah, so that in
scenes of the Resurrection the sarcophagus from which Christ
is emerging looks like Noah's ark.[7] In his version of the story
of Noah and the Deluge, which runs to more than 200 lines in
Books 11 and 12 of *Paradise Lost*, Milton likewise emphasizes
that Noah participated in an act of creation and salvation.
While the Deluge is described imagistically as a reversion to
chaos, the gradual appearance of the dry earth resembles the
emergence of the Creation in Book 7. The account of Noah,
who will "raise another World" (11.877) and from whom "a

second stock [will] proceed" (12.7), typologically resembles the description of the Son as Creator and Redeemer.

Milton closely interrelates these two roles of the Son, so that a description of the one seems designed to recall the other. Commenting on the role of the Redeemer, God the Father foresees that the Son after death will "rise, and rising with him raise / His brethren" (3.296–97). God the Father also prophesies that mankind through the Son "As from a second root shall be restor'd" (3.288). From this perspective the Redemption becomes the second creation, and the typological affinity between the Son and Noah is well defined. At the same time this perspective calls attention to the fallen angels on the burning lake. It thereby develops a view' of Satan's participating in a "second creation and first salvation" (to use D. C. Allen's words) against a framework involving Noah and Christ, whose typological resemblances as creator-figures, as those delivered from death, and as deliverers of others from death, are explained by the Church Fathers and depicted in iconography.

Shortly after he regains consciousness, Satan recognizes that the "fiery Deluge" (1.68) in which he was immersed is beginning to subside. He lifts himself and travels "till on dry Land / He lights" (1.227–28). In the description of the Deluge in Book 11, Noah seeks out land on which the "foot may light" (11.858) until finally "dry ground appears" (11.861). When Satan stands upright on the shore to address the fallen angels, his arms are outstretched and spear uplifted. The *orans* attitude here assumed is also the posture of Noah after the deliverance from the Flood, an attitude suggesting resemblances with the "Risen God," as D. C. Allen remarks (p. 170). "With uplifted hands" (11.863) Noah offers a prayer of thanksgiving for his participation in this "second creation and first salvation." Whereas Noah relates to God with "eyes devout" (11.863), Satan's eyes convey "obdúrate pride and steadfast hate" (1.59) and the resolve to pursue war. To arouse the fallen angels still "covering the Flood" (1.312), Satan calls so loud "that all the hollow Deep / Of Hell resounded" (1.314–15). This act of re-creation and deliverance enables the fallen angels to emerge from the waters of destruction and to escape annihilation. The gradual appearance of the hellish underworld and the revival of the fallen angels—"up they sprung" (1.331)—develop ironic comparisons between Satan and Noah, with whom issuance, birth, and repopulation are continually associated in Books 11 and 12. Many of the same words—"spring," "raise," "issue," and "proceed"— describe the actions of Noah and Satan.

Other images applied to Noah and Satan include those of light and the sun. After the Deluge God's creation reappears under "the clear Sun" (11.844) dispelling clouds and darkness, and an image of light calls attention to Noah's goodness against the depravity of other men: he was "the only Son of light / In a dark Age" (11.808–9). This image, of course, pertains to Christ, who is described as the true bringer of light throughout Milton's poetry and prose. Several scriptural texts provide the basis for this image, including the Old Testament prophecies (in Isaiah, Job, and the Psalms attributed to David) that look forward to the Harrowing of Hell. In Isaiah 9:2, for instance, people walking in the darkness are described as they see a great light. To recount Satan's relationship with the fallen angels, Milton uses similar images. In an environment of darkness, the fallen angels view Satan "above the rest" (1.589) and recognize that "his form had yet not lost / All her Original brightness" (1.591–92). Likened to "the sun new ris'n" or the sun dimmed by eclipse (1.594–99), Satan appeared "Dark'n'd so" to the fallen angels while he "shone / Above them all" (1.599–600). Admittedly, Milton is suggesting that Satan's downfall has resulted in a diminution of former brilliance. But this striking juxtaposition of light and darkness calls attention to the special nature and fullness of Satan's depravity, the extent to which it is held up for the admiration and emulation of the fallen angels, and the manner by which it is visibly imparted to them while they are virtually recreated under his influence. Indeed, the paradoxical image of "Dark with excessive bright" (3.380) describes the Godhead throughout *Paradise Lost*, especially the Son.

These and other images are continually applied to Noah, the Son, and Satan. The essential paradigm of descent and reascent, for example, describes the immersion and emersion of Noah and the ark, but it pertains also to Satan's claim that the fallen angels, having suffered adversity and loss, will "re-ascend / Self-rais'd, and repossess thir native seat" (1.633–34). Where there was darkness, Satan promises light; in place of *tristia,* he brings *gaudium;* for despair, he offers hope. What Satan falsely promises the fallen angels, Christ actually achieves for mankind by His humiliation and exaltation, His Death and Resurrection. In the Descent into Hell, foreshadowed by the darkness and confinement in Noah's ark, Christ delivers and leads forth the souls from captivity and extends the offer of salvation to mankind generally.

The descent into Hell is suggested in the characterization of Noah, who "preach'd / Conversion and Repentance, as to Souls / In Prison under Judgments imminent" (11.723–25). In this adaptation of 1 Peter 3:19, where Christ is described as one who "preached unto the spirits that were in prison," Milton is highlighting resemblances between the judging and preaching of Noah and Christ.[8] Commentary on 1 Peter 3:19 indicates that during the Descent into Hell Christ preached to those very persons who perished in the Flood. In their persistent sinfulness they failed to heed Noah's preaching. Judged to be damned, they suffered death in the Flood, and their souls were consigned to Hell. In preaching to them during his Descent, Christ identifies them as reprobates who deserve continuing punishment. As confronted by Christ during His Descent, the devil is often visualized as a tyrant—either a grotesque monarch of the underworld who subjugates, tortures, and confines the souls of the damned or a monster (Leviathan, a whale, a serpent, or dragon) who holds the captive souls in his mouth, jaws, and teeth. But to those souls whom he will liberate from the tyranny of Satan, Christ preaches a message of hope as a reward for their faithfulness. Those whom He will lead forth from Hell are traditionally compared to the inhabitants of the ark surviving the Flood. The eschatological vision reflected in the preaching and judging of Noah and Christ is related to the Second Coming, when Christ will finally judge and distinguish the saved from the damned. The ironic similarities to Satan's preaching and judging in the hellish underworld of *Paradise Lost* are striking, for Satan also professes to be a deliverer. Those angels who do not heed his preaching will "be for ever fallen" (1.330), consigned to the torment of the "fiery Deluge" (1:68) and restrained in "Adamantine Chains" (1:48). Those angels who respond to his message of hope and follow his lead toward freedom will be saved. For him, God is the tyrant, as Satan iterates again and again in his orations in Books 1, 2, 5, and 6 of *Paradise Lost,* against whom a war of liberation must be pursued. Moloch, one of the fallen angels, calls God "the Torturer" (2.64), Hell "The Prison of his Tyranny" (2.59), and the punished angels "His captive multitude" (2.323). Like Noah and, especially, the Son, who actually experiences the waters of death in order to begin the world anew, Satan provides his followers with the pattern and norm for heroism, whereby humiliation is followed by exaltation, descent by ascent, and patience by victory. For this pattern and norm he, like Christ, is the teacher, witness, and the judge. Both of them, in fact, may be described as St. Paul describes Christ in Colossians 1:18, the "first born of the dead."

Noah also prefigures Christ's role of Judge at the Second Coming, a prefiguration that Christ Himself acknowledges in Matthew 24:35–39 and Luke 17:22–27. This typological similarity is also suggested in 2 Peter 3:3–7, in which the destruc-

tive effect of the Deluge is likened to the conflagration that
will end the world at the eschaton or Second Coming. As the
Judge at the eschaton, Christ will perform and indeed consummate His roles as Redeemer and Creator. Clearly interrelated, all three roles—Judge, Redeemer, and Creator—are
typologically prefigured by Noah and ironically enacted by
Satan in *Paradise Lost*. In leading his followers through the
Deluge, Noah resembles both the victorious Christ descend-
ing into Hell in order to lead forth the "multitude of . . .
redeem'd" (3.260) and the all-judging Christ raising
heavenward the faithful who are to be saved at the Second
Coming (3:333–41). Noah and his family in the ark, which he
constructed "To save himself and household from amidst / A
World devote to universal rack" (11.820–21), also
foreshadow the members of the Christian church.[9] Prefigured
by the appearance of the new world after the Deluge and the
emergence of Noah and his family after the threat of destruction, the Second Coming and its attendant cataclysm will
result in judgment, recreation, salvation, and reward for the
Church Triumphant.

Throughout *Paradise Lost* Milton adapts the account in the
Book of Revelation (chaps. 20–21) to describe the Second
Coming. The archangel Michael explains to Adam that
Christ, having finally defeated Satan, will

> . . . then raise
> From the conflagrant mass, purg'd and refin'd,
> New Heav'ns, new Earth, Ages of endless date
> Founded in righteousness and peace and love,
> To bring forth fruits Joy and eternal Bliss.
>
> (12.547–51).

God the Father, shortly after the Son has volunteered to assume human nature and die in behalf of fallen mankind, states
that the Son "shalt judge / Bad men and Angels, they arraign'd
shall sink / Beneath [his] Sentence" (3.330–32). In addition,

The World shall burn, and from her ashes spring
New Heav'n and Earth, wherein the just shall dwell
And after all thir tribulations long
See golden days, fruitful of golden deeds,
With Joy and Love triumphing, and fair Truth.
Then thou thy regal Sceptre shalt lay by,
For regal Sceptre then no more shall need,
God shall be All in All.

(3.334–41)

In these and other closely related passages, the Second Coming is described as a condition of total destruction, followed by a process of judgment whereby the damned are consumed but the faithful saved, a recreation in which a blissful condition lasting eternally will be enjoyed by the saved, and a virtual union of mankind and the Godhead.

Foreshadowing not only the Paschal Mystery but also the Second Coming and the eschatological vision therein, Noah and the Deluge supply an important context for added understanding of Satan's relationship with the fallen angels and with the characters of Sin and Death in *Paradise Lost*. Like Noah, Satan enacts three roles simultaneously: creator, savior, and judge. According to the norms they themselves embody, Noah and Satan judge and save others. Noah preached and exemplified righteousness, which distinguished those saved from those destroyed; and Satan himself is the consummate manifestation of the sinfulness and depravity in the angels whom he saves from the "fiery Deluge." From those saved from the threat of destruction, the new worlds respectively envisioned by Noah and Satan will be populated.

Described as the first day of the new week, the day after the Sabbath, or simply as the eighth day, the beginning of the new world after the Deluge anticipates the blissful condition that will be enjoyed eternally by those saved, the reward of the Church Triumphant.[10] In his orations to the fallen angels and in his dialogues with Sin (Books 2 and 10), Satan prom-

ises not only ascent from darkness and confinement but also
the founding of a new world. The hellish underworld, which
he already has created, signifies another more lasting kingdom. Assembled in the temple of Pandemonium, the fallen
angels constitute the body of the faithful, the believers of
Satan (a Church Militant), hopeful of salvation and striving
toward it through his effort. His descriptions of the new
world are remarkably analogous to the accounts of the re-
creation that will result from the Second Coming. Having
been persuaded by Satan, Sin provides the key to the gates of
Hell while anticipating that Satan "wilt bring [her] soon / To
that new world of light and bliss, among / The Gods who live
at ease" (2.866–68). Later, in Book 10, as Satan is returning to
Hell after having tempted Eve, he encounters Sin and Death,
who had been following his path through Chaos and toward
the World. He exclaims that he has "made one Realm / Hell
and this World, one Realm, one Continent / Of easy thor-
ough-fare" (10.391–93). When he rejoins the fallen angels,
whom he addresses as "ye Gods" (10.502), he is exultant as he
urges them "to up and enter now into full bliss" (10.503).

Much as the elimination of the sinful world preceded the
effort "To raise another World / From [Noah]" (11.877–78),
so also Satan chooses to create a new domain in the midst of
the destruction carried on by him, by Sin and Death, and by
the fallen angels. Satan asserted that Sin and Death "shall be
fed and fill'd / Immeasurably, all things shall be [their] prey"
(2.843–44). Later, in Book 10, he urges them to make "Man"
(1.401) their "thrall, and lastly kill" (1.402). Of course, the
destruction to be wrought by the fallen angels was described
earlier in the epic, in the catalogue of the pagan deities whom
the epic narrator describes as "Roaming to seek thir prey on
earth" (1.382). The destruction encouraged by Satan is a virtual process of "uncreation," resembling the state of Chaos
that preceded the primal act of Creation and the annihilating
effects of the Deluge.[11] It is a process whereby God's Crea-

tion will become disordered, His creatures consumed, and His immanent presence on earth eradicated. In the midst of this devastation, Satan's new realm will emerge, a realm for which he will serve as creator, judge, and savior, in which the Church Militant will become the Church Triumphant, in which eternal bliss will prevail, in which the power and influence of Hell will extend beyond its confines into the Earth, and in which Sin and Death and the fallen angels will more fully share Satan's triumphal achievement and more completely reflect his corrupting nature.

In *Paradise Lost* Satan's intended process of "uncreation" is likened not only to the state of Chaos and the effects of the Deluge but also to the threats posed by Leviathan. As a recurrent image for Satan in both the Old and New Testaments, Leviathan is described as a voracious sea monster endangering God's creatures by his attempt to consume them, and as threatening God's creation by causing turbulence and upheaval in the waters he inhabits. Iterated in the writings of the Church Fathers, such descriptions of Leviathan similarly appear in imaginative literature—in, for example, the play *Noah's Flood, or the destruction of the world* (1679) by Edward Ecclestone. There Lucifer gives ringing commands to his fellow demons to destroy the ark:

> Ho *Moloch!* loose the Easter Wind, let go,
> *Belial,* the West, both shall together blow,
> You, *Asmoday,* must rule the Southern Wind,
> Ho *Beelzebub!* the stubborn North unbind
> Whilst I and *Satan,* like two mighty Whales,
> Toss up the Ark, with our impetuous Tails.[12]

If, on the one hand, the Flood is divine retribution against the reprobates, it is also the means by which Satan, imaged as Leviathan, will seek to destroy and consume the "remnant" of God's creatures, like Noah and the other inhabitants of the ark, through whom God intends to populate the new world. The upheaval of the sea thrashed by Leviathan and the turmoil of the winds result in confusion, chaos, and the possibility of destruction of God's creatures. The calming of this turbulence, the emergence of dry land, and the beginning of a new society represent the triumph of Creation over Chaos and of God's creatures over Leviathan and the Flood.

Depicting an ark nearly submerged in a raging sea visualizes the imagery of Genesis 6–9, the principal description of the Deluge and Noah's entrance onto dry land. But other scriptural passages describing the threats of Leviathan are also interpreted by the Church Fathers and depicted in iconography in relation to Noah. In such cases Noah's experience of immersion and emersion becomes the prototype for the successful contests of other Old Testament personages against Leviathan, contests prefiguring Christ's Paschal victory. There are no better examples than the interpretations and depictions of Job 40–41, two chapters of Scripture describing how enormous, strong, ferocious, and seemingly indestructible Leviathan is. To combat the monster an effective strategy might be to "draw out Leviathan with a hook, and with a line . . . cast down unto his tongue" (Job 40:20). Among other commentators on this passage, Honorius of Autun and Gregory the Great elaborate the image of fishing, and in iconographic representation of the same passage—in, for instance, *L'Hortus Deliciarum*, an illuminated manuscript of the fourteenth century—God the Father appears as a fisherman.[13] From a pole in His hands, a long line with seven heads pictured along it, including Noah's, descends toward the opened jaws of Leviathan. At the very bottom of the line is Christ crucified, Himself the bait and His cross the hook to catch the monster. The seven patriarchs and prophets of the Old Testament prefigure Christ's entering the jaws of Leviathan and His subsequent emergence. By His Descent into Hell and

Resurrection, Christ fulfills the paradigm of immersion and emersion foreshadowed by His Old Testament precursors.

Iconography depicts many other correlations between Noah's experience of immersion and emersion and the deeds of Old Testament prophets and patriarchs. In the *Biblia Pauperum* the visualization of Jonah being thrown overboard (Jonah 1:15;2:1) shows Leviathan nearby with jaws open and teeth bared. In the depiction of his emergence from Leviathan's jaws (Jonah 2:11), Jonah has his arms upraised in the *orans* posture as he thanks God for deliverance. The land on which he will alight is visible. These visual details alone highlight similarities between Noah and Jonah, and the scriptural passages they depict develop the likenesses even more graphically. Jonah's ship is threatened by a "wroght," "troublous," and "raging" sea (Jonah 1:11–15). Having been thrown overboard and swallowed by the whale, Jonah prays for deliverance. He has been "cast into the bottome in the middes of the sea, and the floods compassed [him] about: all . . . surges, and all . . . waves passed over [him]" (Jonah 2:3).

Leviathan, to which Satan is likened early in the epic, is thus an appropriate image for "uncreation"—for the destruction of Creation Satan plans and the ravenous consumption of God's creatures perpetrated by Sin and Death and by the fallen angels in their guises as pagan deities. Such destruction, moreover, characterizes the periodic upheavals caused by corrupted and fallen men. Milton's interpretation of biblical history in Books 11 and 12 of *Paradise Lost* emphasizes how such figures as the "Giants of mighty Bone" (11.642) slaughtered livestock, razed cities, and "such Massacre / [Made] . . . of thir brethren" (11.679–80). Other examples of corrupted and fallen men include Nimrod, who worked to "dispossess / Concord and law of Nature from the Earth; / Hunting (and Men not Beasts shall be his game) / With War and hostile snare such as refuse / Subjection to his Empire tyrannous"

(12.28–32), and the Egyptian pharaoh, who enslaved the Israelites and "kill[ed] thir infant Males" (12.168). After the devastation that he causes, Nimrod and his followers sought "to build / A City and Tow'r, whose top may reach to Heav'n" (12.43–44). These and other sights of destruction viewed by Adam show the misdeeds of men who, like Satan and the fallen angels, seek to destroy God's Creation and His creatures as a prelude to the formation of the realms they envision.

Divine retribution against these reprobates is remarkably similar, for the Giants perish in the Deluge; the builders of Babel are confused by the various languages they are made to speak—they "see the hubbub strange / And hear the din" (12.60–61); and the sea consumes pharaoh and his cavalry. In all cases imagery of confusion, floodlike destruction, and virtual chaos characterize the divine retribution. Interspersed with the accounts of fallen and corrupt men are commentaries on the "shadowy Types" (12.303), of whom Noah is the first, prefiguring Christ's ministry of Redemption. Reflected in Adam's dream-vision in Books 11 and 12 of the epic, Milton's view of biblical history contrasts the deeds of prophets and patriarchs with the misdeeds of reprobates. Both cyclical and linear, this view of biblical history perceives reenactments of the devastation caused by the reprobates followed by recurrences of the redemption or salvation achieved by God through His chosen ministers. Noah, for instance, begins the "world restor'd" (12.3) immediately after the Giants and other sinful men had become the "world destroy'd" (12.3) in the Flood. Until the Second Coming, when the reprobates will finally be destroyed by the all-judging Son, the *agon* between the Godhead and Satan will be continued on earth between their respective ministers.

From the interrelated perspectives developed in this presentation, Satan throughout *Paradise Lost* is characterized as the demonic counterpart of Noah and of the suffering and triumphant Christ. Evident in these comparisons is Milton's technique of defining the image in relation to the idol, the authentic in relation to the counterfeit, and the hero in relation to the pseudo-hero. It is a technique that suggests definition by logical contraries, a technique that Milton as a logician did know. Just as important, it is a technique that enables Milton to develop his sense of irony to the fullest. The means and manner by which Satan seeks to continue his war against the Godhead are likened to the very means and manner by which his defeat will be achieved. In pursuing victory, Satan is made to enact his own defeat, a defeat prefigured by the Old Testament deeds of Noah, accomplished in the New Dispensation by Christ's Death and Resurrection, and to be confirmed eternally at the Second Coming. The victories over Satan and his ministers by Noah and other Old Testament prefigurations of Christ do teach what has been, is, and will be; but distinctions between history and prophecy are collapsed, so that the "fullness of time" will disclose, paradoxically, what is.

## Notes

1. An earlier, shorter, and somewhat different version of this essay was published as "*Christus Patiens:* The Virtue Patience and *Paradise Lost,* I and II," in *The Triumph of Patience,* ed. Gerald J. Schiffhorst (Gainesville: University Presses of Florida, 1978). For a reprint of the illustration of Jacob dreaming, see James Strachan, *Early Bible Illustrations* (Cambridge: The University Press, 1957), pp. 36–38 and illus. 45.

2. *The Works of John Milton,* ed. F. A. Patterson et al. (New York: Columbia University Press, 1938), 18:240–41. Milton's prose is quoted from this edition, with volume and page numbers cited parenthetically in the text.

3. See Burton O. Kurth, *Milton and Christian Heroism* (Berkeley: University of California Press, 1959), pp. 107–34; John M. Steadman, "The 'Suffering Servant' and Milton's Heroic Norm," *Harvard Theological Review* 54 (1961): 29–43; idem, *Milton and the Renaissance Hero* (Oxford: Clarendon Press, 1967), esp. pp. 30–43.

4. Milton's poetry is quoted from *John Milton: Complete Poetry and Major Prose,* ed. Merritt Y. Hughes (New York: Odyssey Press, 1957).

5. For a discussion of Milton's use of parody as a structural principle, see B. Rajan, "The Cunning Resemblance," in *"Eyes Fast Fixt": Current Perspectives in*

*Milton Methodology, Milton Studies* VII, ed. Albert C. Labriola and Michael Lieb (Pittsburgh, Pa.: University of Pittsburgh Press, 1975), pp. 29–48.

6. Don Cameron Allen, *The Legend of Noah: Renaissance Rationalism in Art, Science, and Letters* (Urbana: University of Illinois Press, 1949), pp. 154, 176.

7. Allen's book is a detailed study of iconographic depictions of Noah. For a brief history of visual representation of Noah, see Allen, *Legend of Noah,* esp. pp. 155–73.

8. Scripture is quoted from the English Geneva Bible of 1560. I have modernized obsolete characters.

9. Allen, *Legend of Noah,* p. 180.

10. For a discussion of the eighth day, see Jean Daniélou, *The Bible and the Liturgy* (South Bend, Ind.: University of Notre Dame Press, 1956), pp. 262–86.

11. For a discussion of "uncreation," see Michael Lieb, *The Dialectics of Creation: Patterns of Birth & Regeneration in Paradise Lost* (Amherst: University of Massachusetts Press, 1970).

12. Quoted by Allen, *Legend of Noah,* p. 153.

13. See Gérard Cames, *Allégories et symboles dans l'Hortus Deliciarum* (Leiden: E. J. Brill, 1971), pp. 40–42 and fig. 35.

PART IV

*The Pictorial Dimension*

# 8

# Milton's Samson and the Iconography of Wordly Vice

## Paul F. Reichardt

AS a seventeenth-century Christian, John Milton had at his disposal a scheme of conventionalized imagery that served to illustrate the themes of Scripture and the trials and triumphs of spiritual life. As a Puritan and an imaginative poet, Milton was also capable of adapting and modifying the emblems known to Chaucer, Spenser, and other antecedent Christian poets in order to suit his own pious views and his sense of literary decorum. Familiarity with traditional iconographic themes in art and literature could therefore prove enlightening to the interpreter of Miltonic texts, and this is the premise for the following discussion of *Samson Agonistes*.

The idea that a seventeenth-century poem like *Samson Agonistes* might contain iconographic elements recast in the form of poetic fiction is strengthened by a glance at the work of Milton's admired predecessor, the "sage and serious poet Spenser."[1] The *Faerie Queene*, for example, fairly bristles with significant examples of visual iconography transformed into narrative detail, as any reading of the episodes of the House of Pride, the House of Holiness, the Cave of Mammon, and the Bower of Bliss will attest. I have in mind here not only the appearance of abstract personifications, such as the seven deadly sins, which parade in the House of Pride, but also the construction of larger scenes that partake of con-

ventionalized form and established significance, such as the
rather pointed correspondence between Guyon's temptation
by Mammon in Book II, canto x, and the temptation of
Christ as recorded in Matthew 4:1–11.[2] The iconographic
threads of Spenser's narrative, by they single detail, individual figure, or complete episode, serve to bind particularized character and action to universal moral themes
that are the driving force of the *Faerie Queene's* structure.[3]

By and large, Milton's poetry shares Spenser's habit of
portraying moral and religous concepts through allusion to
conventionalized form and meaning. *Samson Agonistes,* like
so many other Miltonic works, is an extended allusion to
biblical narrative, with elaboration of the dramatic and em-
pathic possibilities of that narrative. But the design of Samson's story, as it appears in Milton's poem as character, dialogue, and action, is also determined in large measure by a set
of controlling ideas that place the hero squarely within the
context of traditional Christian morality. These controlling
ideas, as we might expect, are traceable to a scriptural source,
but they are also discernible in the poem through imagery and
descriptive detail with iconographic coloring.

The pattern of trial and tribulation endured by Milton's
Samson is clarified by an interesting passage of the poet's *De
Doctrina Christiana.* In the eighth chapter of the first book of
the *Doctrina,* as part of a passage that treats the subject of
temptation to sin, Milton identifies the true spiritual adversaries of mankind by quoting 1 John 2:16: "for all that is in
the world, the lust of the flesh, and the lust of the eyes, and
the pride of life, is not of the Father, but is of the world."[4]
Thus for Milton, as for generations of Christians before him,
this scriptural formula of triple temptation constituted an au-
thoritative description of the human spiritual dilemma: mankind, aspiring to God's love and favor, is beset with the sinis-
ter distractions of "the world."

When visualized, this description of the pious man encompassed by the tempting vices of earthly life became a familiar theme in the moralized art of the Renaissance, from the work of Dürer to the multitude of emblem books produced in this age.[5] The scene itself was portrayed with some variety, of course, with the harrying figures ranging from the deadly sins[6] to allegorizations of the World, Flesh, the Devil, and Death[7] to the scriptural triad of 1 John 2:16 just quoted from Milton's *Doctrina*. It is significant then that Milton chose the triad from 1 John in his prose statement of man's spiritual dilemma rather than other schematizations then current. The import of this choice for *Samson Agonistes* will be considered shortly.

The basic concept of the world and its vices as the Christian's adversary is, however, broader than the confines of a single biblical verse. In fact, within the same epistle in which the triadic scheme of worldly vices appears, we also find the following elaborations: "Love not the world, nor the things that are in the world" (1 John 2:15) and "For whatsoever is born of God overcometh the world; this is the victory that overcometh the world, even our faith" (1 John 5:4). Taken together, these and like biblical maxims constitute a theme-complex that both explains and offers a solution to the Christian's dilemma with worldly temptation. Further, and even more important for an understanding of *Samson Agonistes*, is the fact that this theme-complex generated a vivid and consistent vocabulary of imagery in the visual arts and literature, a circumstance that deserves some emphasis.

A necessary first step in this generation of imagery is agreement on what the triad of worldly vice in 1 John 2:16 refers to. The conventional gloss of the English divine William Tyndale will provide this information:

By the lust of the flesh is understood lechery, which maketh a man altogether a swine. And by the lust of the eyes is understood covetousness, which is the root of all

evil, and maketh to err from the faith. . . . And then followeth pride. Which three are the world, and captains over
all other vices, and occasions of all mischief.[8]

Tyndale, like exegetes before him,[9] assigns to each member of
the triad of 1 John an identity derived from the schema of the
seven deadly sins: the lust of the flesh is clearly lechery, the
lust of the eyes is avarice in all its forms, and the pride of life
is exactly what its name suggests. Tyndale's equation represents the traditional exposition of the text, and thus, in terms
of iconographic potential, emblems of lechery, avarice, and
pride, when collocated in text, plate, or canvas, may justly be
interpreted as an emblem of "the world" and its animosity to
Christian faith and virtue.

The connection of the three worldly vices of 1 John 2:16
with *Samson Agonistes* is established through the conventional portrayal of lechery, covetousness, and pride in Christian iconography. Throughout the discussion that follows I
shall emphasize the correspondence between emblematic detail and the depiction of Milton's characters with two objectives in view. First, I intend to draw tempered conclusions on
the thematics of this correspondence in order to offer a fresh
interpretation of the religious meaning of *Samson Agonistes*.
And second, I should like to further clarify Milton's talent for
poetic accommodation by illustrating the harmony of conventional Christian imagery and Old Testament source material in the dramatic text he has created.

My starting point will be the figure of Manoa. A close
reading of the text supports the idea that Milton has in this
character combined features imposed by his biblical source
material with attributes derived from emblematic portrayals
of worldly vice. For example, the trait of advanced age in
Manoa's physical appearance is, by it very repetition, a key
point in his characterization. He is called "old *Manoa*" (328,
1441), he has "Locks white as down" (327), and the summary

impression of his physique is conveyed by the phrase "cast back with age" (336). Granting the obvious necessity of portraying Samson's father as older than the hero himself, it still seems that the attribute of age is driven home with some urgency in Manoa. Perhaps then the trait itself suggests more than the poet's faithfulness to his scriptural source.

An important clue to the significance of Manoa's advanced age in the light of traditional iconography is given by the words of advice offered by the old man to his son. Manoa's solution to Samson's dilemma is, in a word, *ransom.* The term itself is mentioned no fewer than four times by the old man (484, 606, 1460, 1471), and it takes no special insight to see that Manoa's mind is set, in the words of the poem, on "private reward, for which both God and State . . . easily would set to sale" (1465–66). But Manoa's association with the power of riches and his apparent assumption that everything has its price tag, even human freedom and dignity, goes beyond the words he uses. Iconographically, his most prominent physical feature, advanced age, is a sign of his connection with the lust of the eyes, the vice of avarice. Like "old Manoa," the *senex* figure of medieval and Renaissance emblematic art is consistently portrayed as occupied with and relying on his worldly wealth. Thus while the generalized significance of the "old man" in Scripture is unregenerate human nature (on authority of Romans 6:6, Ephesians 4:22, and Colossians 3:9), the place of the *senex* in iconography is often more narrowly defined. In the emblematic theme of the "ages of man," in which each stage of human life is assigned a characterizing vice, the *senex* figure is consistently allotted the sin of covetousness. The literary authority for this equation is traceable to the discussion of *avaritia senilis* in Cicero's *De Senectute.*[10] Though Cicero stops short of identifying covetousness as the predominant vice of old age, his remarks are taken as warrant for such an identification by medieval writers such as Pope Innocent II in his influential *De Miseria*

*Humane Conditionis.*[11] Numerous examples of the perpetua-
tion of the *avaritia senilis* theme in the Renaissance are provided by the visual arts. A typical portrayal is that found in a
set of late-seventeenth-century engravings designed and published in France by Nicholas Guerard. Here four ages of man
are represented, each according to a traditional scheme.
Youth is an adolescent who pauses reflectively before several
different paths (each standing for a possible career or way of
life); adulthood is a robust reveler who holds a bottle and
wineglass; middle age is a figure weighed down by the cares
of business and family; and old age is a stooped fellow who
hobbles along clutching a large money chest.[12] A corroborative treatment of the *senex* figure may be seen in the engravings published under the title *Aetates Hominem secundum
Anni Tempora* (Cologne, 1599). Here old age is depicted as
an elderly figure beside a coffer filled with coins and jewels,
with a wolf (probably an emblem of avarice in itself)[13] de-
vouring a lamb portrayed in the background of the scene.[14]
But perhaps the most persuasive evidence of the iconographic
significance of Milton's Manoa and his trust in wealth is sup-
plied by the poetry of Spenser, whose portrait of the emblematic figure of Avarice in the *Faerie Queene*'s House of Pride
(Book I, canto iv) is in full accord with the tradition of *avaritia senilis*. Avarice is portrayed as "uppon a camell loaden
all with gold; / Two iron coffers hong on either side, / With
precious metall full," and his age is explicitly recorded: "His
life was nigh unto deaths dore yplaste."[15]

Spenser's emblematic *senex* goes some distance toward establishing the iconographic potential of Milton's "old
Manoa" as one tainted with the worldly lust of the eyes. Yet
sensitive readers will be quick to point out that Manoa is
portrayed as neither a tempting demon nor a hollow emblem.
And of course they are correct. Milton's Manoa, though he
trusts in the power of worldly riches, is nevertheless willing
to part with his wealth to aid his son:

No, I am fixt not to part hence without him.
For his redemption all my Patrimony,
If need be, I am ready to forego
And quit: not wanting him, I shall want nothing.

(1481–84)

This selflessness is a significant and particularizing difference
between Manoa and the avaricious *senex* figure. It suggests
that Milton meant to create a character who was at once
emblematic in his role as the hero's interlocutor and more
than an emblem as Samson's father. As unwitting spokesman
for a specific worldly vice, Manoa is cut after the mold of
Spenser's figure of Avarice and his visual counterparts in the
engravings of Guerard and the *Aetates Hominem secundum
Anni Tempora.* He thus illustrates a dimension of iconographic vice that is neither easily recognized nor casually rejected by the hero. Samson must respectfully but firmly refuse a father's solicitous offer of worldly wealth as a solution
to his dilemma, and by so doing he dismisses the first of the
scriptural triad from 1 John 2:16 to appear in the poem.

To turn next to the figure of Dalilah. It would hardly be
controversial to suggest that she is an image of the lust of the
flesh or lechery.[16] In her own words, the motive for her
betrayal of Samson was fear of losing his physical attentions
(790–96), and in this same passage she speaks in almost pa-
tently iconographic terms when she describes the jealous passions of sensual love as holding "powerful . . . sway / in
human hearts" (791–92). In a sense, the image of Love "holding sway" or tyrannically ruling the wills of infatuated men
colors the whole Dalilah episode of *Samson Agonistes.* At one
point, for example, Dalilah remarks that she desires to make
Samson "Mine and Love's prisoner, not the *Philistines'* "
(808), which effectively explains her desire to subject the hero
to the spiritual bondage of a life devoted to sensual
gratification in place of his present physical slavery to his

enemies. Samson has no interest in such a change of masters,
however, and he tells her so. But behind his overt rejection of
Dalilah's offer lie significant iconographic overtones.

In representations of the "triumph of love" theme, a virile
male is often shown bound or trodden underfoot by the
figures of Venus or Cupid. And when these portrayals include biblical or historical "victims" of fleshly passions, the
figure of Samson is often prominently displayed. The literary
*locus classicus* for Samson's association with the scene of
Love's triumph is the *Trionfi* of Francesco Petrarca:

> See then how love in evil cruelty
> Overcame David, leading him to a sin
> He was to weep for in a dark retreat.
> See how the cloud of love likewise obscures
> The clear fame of the wisest of his sons,
> Leading him far astray from the Lord above.
> Of another son, who loves and yet loves not,
> Tamar, o'erwhelmed by her disdainful grief,
> Turns in complaint to her brother Absalom.
> Closely beyond her, Samson you may see,
> Stronger than he is wise, who foolishly
> Laid low his head upon a hostile lap.[17]

In the visual arts an appropriate example of this same motif is
provided by a northern Italian fresco now in the Louvre,
which is cited by Panofsky in *Studies in Iconology*.[18] Here
Venus is depicted with her most illustrious victims: Achilles,
Paris, Troilus, Tristram, Lancelot, and, of course, Samson.
Samson's reputation as a sort of "textbook case" of Love's
tyranny sheds new light on Dalilah's offer of sensual
gratification in Milton's poem. Through this offer Milton has
provided his hero with an opportunity to exorcise a negative
dimension of his traditional reputation, his shameful defeat at
the hands of the lust of the flesh, and thus establish by his
rejection of that same lust the idea of hard-won triumph over

one of the world's temptations. The metamorphosis of Samson from victim to victor implied by the iconographic overtones of the Dalilah episode also anticipates the hero's triumph at the end of the poem. Victory over the spiritual enemy of worldly lust presages victory over Samson's physical enemies, the Philistines.

The use of the figure of Dalilah as apologist for the worldly vice of carnality is also consonant with iconographic conventions. Milton's portrait of her rather faithfully reflects the emblems of fleshly lust found in the moralized art of this day. In the poem, she is "bedeckt, ornate, and gay" (712), with "scent of odorous perfume / Her harbinger" (720–21), and it is just such finery that usually identifies the traditional figure of fleshly temptation in visual iconography. For example, the manual of moral emblems entitled *Veridicus Christianus* [19] contains a plate in which a kneeling Christian is tempted by a female figure with bare breasts, a cushion symbolizing idleness on her head, and a hand that extends a flower toward the averted gaze of the righteous man.[20] This figure is specifically identified with the inscription "Caro," the flesh. A similar treatment may be seen in a sixteenth-century woodcut by Cornelius Anthonisz, which depicts a scene that includes a prodigal son (the label is *filius prodigus*) dining with a group of figures, one of whom is an ornately dressed woman who shares a cup of wine with him; again the elegant female is labeled "Caro."[21] The banquet pictured is meant to represent the temptations of worldly living, especially those involving bodily pleasure (using consumption of food and drink as a convenient metaphor for indulgence in all forms of sensual gratification). Milton's Dalilah is the literary offspring of these Caro figures, and her significance in the moral drama of *Samson Agonistes* is closely tied to the meanings established by her emblematic forebears.

If we recall once more our touchstone text in 1 John 2:16, it is obvious that the character Milton invented especially for his poem, the "giant *Harapha* of *Gath*" (1068), has an iconographic identity akin to the last of the worldly vices mentioned there, the pride of life. This identity is not difficult to validate in the details of the text when we remember that the primary attributes of Harapha are imposing physical size and a temperament of "defiance" (1073). A corroborative impression is provided by the words of the Chorus, which refers to him as "proud" (1069), and those of Samson, who calls him a "vain boaster" (1227). Harapha's true character is, of course, also suggested by the fact that although he is angered by the "dishonors" heaped upon him by Samson and the Chorus, he cravenly withdraws from the hero's presence without accepting Samson's challenge to combat. Given these characteristics, it would seem that Harapha is, in appearance at least, an appropriate incarnation of the "pride of life," which 1 John identifies as the third component of the worldly temptations.

But lest we take Harapha's iconographic identity too lightly and thereby miss the full significance of Milton's development of this character, let us look more carefully at what is meant by the phrase *pride of life.* Although Milton did not find Harapha in the account of Samson's life as narrated in the Book of Judges, he could have found a prototype for his haughty giant elsewhere in the Old Testament. Genesis 6:4, for example, speaks of "giants in the earth" in antediluvian times, and a rather traditional interpretation of this reference and the following verses on the "wickedness of man" (6:5) is provided by John Calvin's commentaries on the Book of Genesis:

> they were ferocious tyrants, who separated themselves from the common rank. Their first fault was pride; because relying on their own strength, they abrogated to themselves more than was due. Pride produced contempt of God, because, being inflated by arrogance, they began to shake off every yoke. At the same time, they were also

disdainful and cruel toward men; because it is not possible that they, who would not bear to yield obedience to God, should have acted with moderation toward men. . . . Nor is it to be doubted, that they had something more excellent than the common people, which procured for them favour and glory in the world. Nevertheless, under the magnificent title of heroes, they cruelly exercised dominion, and acquired power and fame for themselves, by injuring and oppressing their brethren. And this was the nobility of the world.[22]

There is, of course, much in these remarks with which Milton would have agreed. There is no need to argue that Milton read this passage, however; it is sufficient to point out that this and various other commentaries on the giants of Genesis laid the groundwork for the traditional image of pride as a giant in iconographic art and literature, and that this association of imposing physical size with worldly vanity colored any late Renaissance portrait of a giant such as Harapha.

Clearly, Milton's Harapha is akin to the giants of Genesis; he has "glory in the world" (to use Calvin's term) as they do. Like them, he is arrogant and contemptuous of God (he says, for example, "Presume not on thy God, whate'er he be," line 1156). Further, the poem makes it abundantly clear that the giant's visit to Samson involves "injuring and oppressing" the blind Hebrew hero. Such conduct is "worldly" in the most derogatory sense of the term, for only corrupt earthly opinion would consider such brute instincts as a sign of honor.

The idea that Milton may have cast his giant in the mold provided by the traditional iconography of human pride becomes even more plausible when we recall that Edmund Spenser also used the image of the giant to create an icon of pride in Book 1 of the *Faerie Queene*. Spenser's Orgoglio (the Italianate name itself means pride) is described as "an hideous geaunt, horrible and hye" who is "puft up with emptie wynd,

and fild with sinfull cryme." In addition, his arrogance is
apparent from Spenser's statement "through arrogant delight
/Of the high descent whereof he was yborne, / And through
presumption of his matchlesse might, / All other powres and
knighthood he did scorne."[23]

And just as Milton's Harapha is related to Spenser's Orgoglio through common reference to iconographic tradition,
the import of the two figures in their respective works is
similar. It may be argued, I think, that Milton intends his
hero to see in Harapha an image of what he himself once was,
just as the Redcrosse Knight is laid low in Spenser's poem by
his own vanity (he encounters Orgoglio just after leaving the
House of Pride). Samson himself refers to his former arrogance ("like a petty God / I walked about admir'd of all and
dreaded / On hostile ground" [529–31]), and thus we may see
in Samson's challenge to Harapha the hero's rejection of his
own faults. This rejection also defines him as delivered from
the last of the three worldly vices that threaten his virtue, the
pride of life. Yet the "pride of life" is no hollow phrase in
*Samson Agonistes;* it walks, talks, jeers, and threatens in the
person of the bully Harapha. But like most bullies (and most
vain and pretentious people), Harapha may be deflated by
resolute honesty and courage, in this case on the part of Milton's hero. With this deflation comes the completion of Samson's moral triumph over the worldly attitudes that dominate
each of his interlocutors in the poem. Moreover, it is the
moral "victory" that prepares the hero for his final combat
with his fleshly adversaries, the assembled Philistine
populace.

Three rather distinct impressions about *Samson Agonistes*
emerge from a survey of its relation to the traditional iconography of worldly vice. First, the fact that the imagery of the
lust of the eyes, the lust of the flesh, and the pride of life is
present in the poem offers at least the beginning of a solution
to the problem of why Milton invented the figure of

Harapha. In order to complete a portrait of the world and its false allure of possessions, pleasure, and pride, an image of human vanity was needed to complement Manoa and Dalilah. Harapha the giant obviously provides this complement; his presence in the poem finishes out the triadic scheme of worldly vice cited in 1 John 2:16 and incarnated by Samson's interlocutors in the poem.

The second impression that emerges from the presence of the iconography of worldly vice is that this iconography throws into relief an essential "idea" that is signified by Samson and his three visitors in the poem. By rejecting the advice and threats of Manoa, Dalilah, and Harapha, Samson has in effect overcome the vices of covetousness, lechery, and pride, and, in so doing, in biblical terms, he has also overcome the "world" itself, thus realizing the promise of 1 John 5:4: "For whatsoever is born of God overcometh the world: and this is the victory that overcometh the world, even our faith." This then is the "idea" that the poem dramatizes, the Christian's struggle against a hostile world, and this concept of Samson's heroism is in full accord with his identity as a "hero of the faith" as set forth in the eleventh chapter of Hebrews. The moral triumph of Milton's Samson over emblematic vice in the poem foreshadows the Christian's victory over the world through faith and thus serves as an exhortation to perseverance and patience in the face of spiritual trials.[24]

And finally, the third and perhaps most interesting of the impressions to emerge from the study of the iconography of worldly vice in *Samson Agonistes* is the light it sheds on Milton's art of characterization. Starting with familiar biblical names and commonplace iconographic details, Milton has breathed "life" and a sense of everyday immediacy into one of the most trite metaphors of his own and previous Christian ages: the spiritual combat waged by the virtuous soul against the world. Some eighty years earlier Edmund Spenser had undertaken a similar task in the lofty allegory of Book I of the

*Faerie Queene.* Yet when Milton's Samson, Manoa, Dalilah, and Harapha are set beside their Spenserian counterparts such as Avarice and Orgoglio, or beside the emblematic figures of moralized visual art, it is clear that Milton's characters, though basically faithful to iconographic conventions, possess a vivid sense of particularity that is missing from their counterparts. Milton's way, for all his admiration of the earlier poet, is not Spenser's way. His emphasis on dramatic detail and coloring, as well as his insistence that biblical characters and ideas correlate with life as it was lived by the seventeenth-century Christian, led Milton to create texts that were simultaneously emblematic and verisimilitudinous. This synchronic momentum is among the most impressive features of Milton's religious and literary vision.

# Notes

1. The descriptive phrase is from *Areopagitica,* where Milton also remarks that Spenser is "a Better teacher than Scotus or Aquinas." See *The Works of John Milton,* ed. F. A. Patterson et al., (New York: Columbia University Press, 1933), 4:311. The edition of *Samson Agonistes* cited throughout is *John Milton: Complete Poems and Major Prose,* ed. Merritt Y. Hughes (New York: Odyssey Press, 1957) pp. 531–93.

2. See. R. Durling, "The Bower of Bliss and Armida's Palace," *Comparative Literature* 6(1954): 335–47.

3. See further Rosemond Tuve, *Allegorical Imagery: Some Medieval Books and Their Posterity* (Princeton, N.J., Princeton University Press, 1966), pp. 31–33.

4. *The Works of John Milton,* 15:72f.

5. See the discussion of Dürer's "Knight, Death, and Devil" in Erwin Panofsky, *The Life and Art of Albrecht Dürer* (Princeton: Princeton University Press, 1943; reprint 1955), p. 153f. For an introduction to emblems on this theme, see Samuel C. Chew, *The Pilgrimage of Life,* (New Haven, Conn.: Yale University Press 1962), pp. 70–78.

6. Cf. "The Temptation of St. Anthony" by a follower of Hieronimus Bosch, now in the Colonna Gallery in Rome, and the painting on the same subject by David Teniers now in the Prado (see Chew, *Pilgrimage of Life,* p. 82f).

7. E.g., "The Christian Knight" theme as rendered by the early seventeenth-century engravers Thomas Cecill in Joseph Fletcher's *The History of the Perfect-Cursed-Blessed Man* (London, 1628; see Chew, *Pilgrimage of Life,* p. 76 f. and fig. 73), and John Payne on the title page of John Downame's *The Christian Warfare against the Devil, World and Flesh* (London, 1634; see Chew, *Pilgrimage of Life,* p. 77 and fig. 74). For further examples, see Chew, *Pilgrimage of Life,* fig. 69–78.

8. *The Exposition of the Fyrst Epistle of Seynt John* (1531) in *English Reformers*, ed. T. H. L. Parker, The Library of Christian Classics, (Philadelphia: Westminster Press, 26:117 f.

9. For a survey of medieval treatments of this scheme, see Donald R. Howard, *The Three Temptations: Medieval Man in Search of the World* (Princeton, N.J.: Princeton University Press, 1966), pp. 43–75.

10. XVII 65. See *Cicero: De Senectute, De Amicitia, De Divinatione*, ed. and trans. William Armistead Falconer (Cambridge, Mass.: Harvard University Press [Loeb Series], 1923).

11. I.10.i. See the translation of this work in *Two Views of Man*, trans. Bernard Murchland (New York: F. Ungar Publishing Company. 1966), p. 11.

12. See Chew, *Pilgrimage of Life*, figs. 112–15.

13. Cf. Dante's *Inferno*, Canto I, ll. 19–60, where a she-wolf is described in the following terms: "a she-wolf which appeared in its leanness to be charged with all cravings and which has already made many live in wretchedness. This last put such heaviness on me by the terror which came forth from its looks that I lost hope of the ascent; and like one who rejoices in his gains and when the time comes that makes him a loser has all his thoughts turned to sadness and lamentation, such did the restless beast make me, coming against me and driving me back step by step to where the sun is silent" (John Donaldson Sinclair translation; London: John Lane, 1939).

14. Chew, *Pilgramage of Life*, p. 162 f.

15. See stanzas xxvii, 11.2–4 and xxvii, 1.1. The edition cited is *The Complete Poetical Works of Spenser*, ed. R. E. Neil Dodge (Boston, Mass.: Houghton Mifflin Company, 1936).

16. Yet F. Michael Krouse in his study *Milton's Samson and the Christian Tradition* (Princeton N.J.: Princeton University Press, 1949; reprint ed. New York: Octagon Books 1974) aligns her with "the world" (p. 131), using the traditional scheme of "the world, the flesh, and the Devil," instead of that found in 1 John 2:16 and Milton's own *De Doctrina*. For Krouse it is Manoa who represents "the Flesh" (p. 126). This interpretation contradicts the clear emphasis in Milton's text on Dalilah's fleshy appeal and is the result of Krouse's assumption that Milton's vision of Samson must be indebted to the "World, Flesh, and Devil" formula of vice. Yet the evidence of iconographic influence on the poem's descriptive detail points toward the scheme of 1 John. What is more, it is worth noting that although the "World, Flesh, and Devil" scheme is indeed common enough in the spiritual writing of the later Middle Ages and Renaissance, it nowhere appears as a formula in Milton's poetry or prose.

17. *The Triumph of Love*, in *The Triumphs of Petrarch*, trans. Ernest Hatch Wilkins (Chicago: University of Chicago Press, 1962), 3:21.

18. (New York: Oxford University Press: 1939; reprint ed. New York: Harper & Row: 1962), p. 115, n. 65.

19. (Antwerp, 1601). See Chew, *Pilgrimage of Life*, pp. 73–75.

20. Chew, *Pilgrimage of Life*, p. 75 and fig. 70.

21. Ibid., p. 94 and fig. 77.

22. Commentaries on the *First Book of Moses Called Genesis*, trans. John King (Grand Rapids, Mich.: W. B. Eerdmans Publishing Co., 1948), 1:246.

23. Canto 7, stanzas 7–10.

24. For a parallel view of the heroism of Milton's Samson, developed from a theological rather than an iconographic perspective, see John M. Steadman, "Faithful Champion: The Theological Basis of Milton's Hero of Faith," *Anglia* 77(1959):12–28.

PART V

*The Literary Dimension*

# 9

# Milton and the Roman de la Rose: Adam and Eve at the Fountain of Narcissus

Edward Sichi, Jr.

> O, Man! See yourself in this
> Three-fold mirror and you will be
> displeased with yourself. Three-fold
> is the mirror in which you ought to
> look: the mirror of the Holy Scriptures,
> the mirror of nature, and the mirror
> of creatures. All these show you what
> you ought to be. Hence, in the mirror
> of the Scriptures you see your present
> state; in the mirror of creatures you
> see yourself as a wretched one; and
> in the mirror of your human nature
> you judge yourself as guilty.
> —Alanus de Insulis (1114–1203),
> *Summa de Arte Predicatoria*[1]

The *Roman de la Rose* is among the most influential works of the late Middle Ages and the Renaissance. The indebtedness of succeeding authors to the *Roman* is inestimable. It is, as it were, the *ur*-text for most of the grand Renaissance epics. Although scholars have long recognized the influence of the *Roman* upon *Paradise Lost*, recent scholarship has neither documented these influences nor interrelated the gardens of the two poems.[2] In discounting the dependence of *Paradise Lost* on the *Roman,* we can cite differences in time, place, and language, Milton's antipathy to things French, and the decidely different tone of the two works. However, the two authors *do* share a common background. Both, for example, knew intimately such literary techniques as the dream-vision, the psychomachia, the quest motif. They also made use of Christian iconography and typology. Moreover, Milton understood French, read widely in French authors, traveled in France, and knew the *Roman de la Rose* at least through Chaucer's incomplete but literal translation. Not only does Milton mention Chaucer's *Romaunt* in his *Commonplace Book,* but also he cites the same work in conjunction with a discussion of *Nobilitas.*[3] Interestingly, both of these entries were made in the early 1640s at a time when Milton was in "the process of preparation for *Paradise Lost.*"[4]

If a major theme of *Paradise Lost* and the *Roman de la Rose* is love, including the proper relationship between man and woman and their proper relationship with God, the similarity between these poems is even more evident. Although the belief that love is of central importance to the *Roman* is not new, few critics have seen love as a major controlling aspect of *Paradise Lost.* However, in "The Metaphor of Inspiration in Paradise Lost," Shawcross states that "love is, I believe, the theme of the poem, [and] it is natural that the basic image pattern derive from the nature of Love."[5] Barry Edward Gross also notes the thematic importance of love to *Paradise Lost* when he says that the dominant theme of the poem is the "difference between a true and a false *love* lying in the contrast of the theocentric and selfless love of Christ and the egocentric and selfish love of Adam and Eve."[6] The *Roman* is, of course, of prime importance among literary accounts of love, the source of much of the allegory, philosophy, and imagery used by authors during the late Middle Ages and the Renaissance. Few will dispute its prominence or its influence for two centuries after its completion, and fewer still will deny its serious and didactic approach to the problems of love. This discussion, therefore, will emphasize the importance of the theme of love in *Paradise Lost* and the *Roman*, and will also note how the use of scenes, characters, and ideas continually highlight this theme. In particular, the treatment given by both authors to the scene of a reflecting fountain and to the dream-vision framework will be considered. Other similarities will be noted when they seem appropriate and illuminating.

Early in the *Roman* Guillaume writes that its pages will enclose "al the arte of loue," and says that the matter is "bone e nueue," an early clue to the ironic and satiric mode of the poem because this art of love is (outwardly at least) neither good nor new as it is presented in the *Roman*.⁷ The art of love had consistently been part of Western literature at least since Ovid. Jean later continues the idea when he says that the poem "is but written for instruction's sake" (70.56). In *Paradise Lost* didacticism is likewise evident. Every reader remembers Milton's famous lines that state that the poem will "assert Eternal Providence / And justify the ways of God to men" (1.25–26), but few seem to note how frequently love is the subject of the poem. The poem opens with the cataclysmic humbling of the self-loving Lucifer, who puts love of self above love of God. In a series of parodies the reader watches Lucifer lust after his own begotten daughter (Sin), who gives birth to Satan's son-grandson. This blasphemous trio sets up an anti-kingdom in the nether world and plans to rain destruction upon mankind. These actions parody those of the Trinity and also insidiously parallel the relationship between Adam and Eve. Such parodies abound in *Paradise Lost*. Consider the following lines spoken by Sin:

> O Father, what intends Thy hand, she cri'd,
> Against thy only Son? What fury O Son,

> Possesses thee to bend that mortal Dart
> Against thy Father's head?
>
> (2.727–30)[8]

Milton ingeniously develops such parodic resemblances throughout *Paradise Lost,* as he reveals a loving, selfless response in Christ's services to the Father and the selfless laying aside of the Godhead to become man. These actions contrast with Lucifer's haughty pride and jealousy toward Christ, his lustful relationship with Sin, and his distasteful lowering and imbruting himself to baser forms, not because of love but, rather, enmity. The transmogrification reaches its nadir when he grovels on his belly as a serpent. Similar parallels and parodies also exist in the *Roman* to highlight and emphasize nearly identical themes. One such example of a lowering that is brought about by self-love and not humility occurs when the Lover is wounded by the God of Love:

> Than I was hurte thus in stounde,
> I fell downe platte vnto the grounde.
> Myn herte fayled and fainted aye
> And longe tyme in swoune I laye.
>
> (1733–36)

In addition, the entire travesty of the pains of love, followed by the Lover's vassalage to the God of Love, his denial of Reason's pleas, and even the language that describes his fall, reveal Guillaume's parodic intent:

> 'Ah, sir, for Goddes loue, sayd I,
> 'Er ye passe hens, ententyfely
> Your commaundements to me ye say,
> And I shal kepe hem, if I may;
> . . . . . . . . . . . . . . . . . . . . . . . .
> Wherfore I praye you entierly,

With al myne herte, me to lere,
That I trespace in no manere."

(2135–44)

Another obvious analogue to the Lover's corruption at the
hands of the God of Love is Pygmalion's self-enthrallment in
falling in love with a statue. Within eleven lines (97.14–25),
Jean describes this infatuation of Pygmalion's with these
words: "gazed entranced," "dream," "an image," "love sick-
ness," and "my senses failing." Pygmalion also says that
"Narcissus fell in love with his own face; / Nor ever could
recover, but expired. . . . At least I am less foolish than was
he, / For I the object of my love can touch" (97.47–51). Jean,
in linking his section of the *Roman* to Guillaume's, reiterates
the theme of the great poem—illusionary love, which debases
with its enthrallment, burns without assuaging, and falsely
imitates true, other-directed love. These scenes closely parallel in intent Milton's depiction of the fealty paid to Satan by
the rebel angels, Eve's admiration of her reflection, the Serpent's adulation of Eve, Eve's, then Adam's, obeisance to the
Tree, and Adam's and Eve's resultant "amorous play."

A discussion of love in the *Roman* must include the Fountain of Narcissus, a central image of the poem. I believe that
the scene that shows Eve's response to her water-reflected
image in the Garden of Eden closely parallels the actions at
the Fountain of Narcissus. Eve's response gives the reader an
important key to understanding the relationship of Adam and
Eve; Adam and Eve's relationship with God and with Satan;
and the reader's relationship with the characters, the narrator,
and, finally, with God. An analysis of the Narcissistic episodes in both poems will, I hope, indicate more exactly what
Milton means by his famous "justification" of God's ways. It
will reveal, for instance, that *Paradise Lost* is an interpretation
of love, or the art of love, incorporating much of the setting,

imagery, allegory, and philosophy utilized four centuries earlier by Guillaume de Lorris and Jean de Meun.

To discuss the art of love, the authors of the *Roman*, following the tradition of much literature of the Middle Ages,
use allegorical example. Although the Middle Ages provides
hundreds of examples of didactic literature, allegorical interpretation was not original with the writers of the Middle
Ages. Jewish commentators on the Bible before the birth of
Christ frequently used allegorical exegesis to explain and
comment on the stories in the Bible and to show a relationship with its readers. The early Church Fathers were not lax
in following these leads, and soon allegorical interpretation
became an accepted mode in ecclesiastical and literary
works.[9] Recently, Stanley Fish has attempted to show that
the true center of *Paradise Lost* is the reader's consciousness
of the poem's personal relevance.[10] The poem develops such a
response in the reader by allowing him to face his own corruption and by inviting him to cooperate with the intention of
the poem to effect his regeneration. Large sections of *Paradise
Lost* (especially, according to Fish, the center sections, Books
4 to 9) are irrelevant as determiners of the crisis of the Fall.
Similarly, critics have noted the seeming irrelevance of sections of the *Roman* (especially in Jean's continuation) to the
actual seduction of the Rose. If, however, the *Roman* is to be
considered a *primer* of love, both human and divine, then
these irrelevancies must have meaning—if not concerning the
seduction of the Rose, then for the response evoked in the
reader. Through the "irrelevant" middle books of *Paradise
Lost*, argues Fish, a reader is given a series of "interpretative
choices" in the form of words and phrases suggestive of earlier points in the poem; it is here, he says, that the reader
gains psychological insight from his own juxtaposition of
these similarities between and among sections of the poem.
Fish believes, moreover, that the reader does the work, not
the poem. I believe that Guillaume and Jean used this method

of suggestive, interpretative choices centuries before Milton. Of course, allegory, by juxtaposing fictional figures and actions with human conduct or experience, allows the reader to gain psychological insights in a manner similar to Fish's theory about *Paradise Lost*. But the *Roman* just as fully participates in offering the reader "interpretative choices." Large sections of the poem (i.e., Reason's lessons, Nature's exposition, and the short "scenes" within these sections—notably the tale of Pygmalion and the description of the Park of the Good Shepherd) are "irrelevant" in helping to create or resolve the crisis between the Lover and his Rose. As in *Paradise Lost*, this particular seduction or "fall" is well known, much rehearsed, and irreversible—and decidedly "nontragic." Rarely are seductions the stuff from which tragedy is woven. Milton seemed to reflect these views when he shaped (or reshaped) his material into epic (but not tragic) proportions; Guillaume and Jean, in reshaping the story of the Fall, distilled it into the essence of romance, a choice wisely rejected by Milton (consider his "Arthuriad").[11]

An example of an "interpretative choice" will illustrate how it is the purpose of both poems to reveal to the reader his own corruption and to invite him to effect his own regeneration. Again, both poets choose nearly identical patterns in order to develop their respective themes. In Book 4 of *Paradise Lost*, for example, we find the justly famous fountain scene where Eve becomes enamored of her own reflection. Several commentators have noted the similarities between this scene and Guillaume's Fountain of Narcissus; few have noted the constant reverberations or suggestive reiteration of elements involved in these treatments of the same theme. Here is Milton's scene (italics added):

> [Eve:]  As I bent down to look, just opposite,
>     *A Shape within the wat'ry gleam appear'd*
>     Bending to look on me, *I started back,*

*It started back,* but pleas'd I soon return'd,
Pleas'd it return'd as soon *with answering looks*
Of sympathy and love; *there I had fixt*
*Mine eyes* till now, and *pin'd with vain desire,*
Had not a voice thus warn'd me, What thou seest,
*What there thou seest fair Creature is thyself,*
With thee it came and goes: but follow me,
And I will bring Thee where *no shadow stays*
They coming, and thy soft embraces . . .
. . . . . . . . . . . . . . . . . . . . . . . . . . . . . . . . .
Til I espi'd thee [Adam] . . .
. . . . . . . . . . . . . . . . . . . . . .
Less winning soft, less amiably mild,
Than that *smooth wat'ry image;* back I turn'd.
(4.460–80)

Later, the reader discovers the following lines, which show
Satan discovered while inspiring Eve (italics added):

him there they found
Squat *like a Toad,* close at the ear of *Eve;*
Assaying by his Devilish art to reach
The organs of her Fancy, and with them forge
*Illusions* as he list, *Phantasms and Dreams,*
Or if, inspiring venom, he might taint
Th' animal spirits that from pure blood arise
Like gentle breaths from Rivers pure, Thence raise
At least distemper'd, discontented thoughts,
*Vain hopes, vain aims, inordinate desires*
Blown up with high conceits *ingend'ring pride.*
. . . . . . . . . . . . . . . . . . . . . . . . . . . . . . . . . . .
*up he starts*
Discover'd and surpris'd . . .
. . . . . . . . . . . . . . . . . . . . . . .
*So started up* in *his own shape* the Fiend.
(4.799–819)

When the reader is confronted with passages like these (and there are many), he can remember the similar words, phrases, images. The mirror image is foremost. Are these complementary scenes a recasting of Ovid's story? Or are they a replay of the famous fountain in the *Roman*? Perhaps they are representative of the biblical glass through which we see darkly. Or perhaps our attention should focus upon Protean imagery; the insistence upon shape, watery image, and shadow in both passages is persuasive. But since the discussion of love (human and divine) is, after all, the purpose of this episode, should the reader consider the Platonic "two-in-one" theory with all of its involvement in Courtly Love and Renaissance literature? Milton may also be referring the reader to the medieval *speculum*, or mirror of self-knowledge, to which the epigraph to this chapter refers. Then, too, the reader should take into account the sin of self-love, or pride, which caused Lucifer's fall and will cause the fall of Adam and Eve, all three self-deluded and self-enthralled. And, iconographically, these passages could relate to the mirror of *Luxuria*, which promises just such "Vain hopes, vain aims, inordinate desires." Or does the image refer to the mirror or well of the Virgin Mary, who will reflect not a false shadow but a Sun, not a moment's bliss but an eternity in heaven?

In considering these passages, one should accordingly note the parallelism and repetition of phrases ascribed to both Eve and Satan. For example, when Eve espies her image, she says, "I started back, / It started back . . . [and finally] back I turned." In the passage where the transmogrified Satan is discovered, the reader is told that "up he starts / . . . / So started up in his own shape." The close resemblance, structurally and grammatically, not only of the two scenes but also of their images and meanings is meaningful. But it is the reader who is the wiser; none of this image-juggling or play of ideas makes Eve or Satan any wiser; none of it is done for their benefit; none of it adds to the poignancy or to the tragedy as they head toward their predefined and prefigured falls. Milton compares Eve's actions to Satan's, his duplicity to her imminent duplicity; his proud self-love to her perilous interaction with her own reflection and the resulting effects of self-enthrallment, lust, and seduction. When the reader notes these comparisons, he can then respond accordingly. For, after all, this is the tale of the Fall of Man, and each man, while reading *Paradise Lost,* can take warning and extricate himself from the false illusions and snares of the world.

The *Roman* displays similar structural resemblances in relation to the use of the mirror image. Jean de Meun contrasts his Fountain in the Park of the Good Shepherd with Guillaume's Mirror Perilous from the opening pages of the poem. If we keep in mind that the Lover is admitted into the Garden of Deduit by Idleness, frequently depicted iconographically as *Luxuria,* who "had [in honde] a gay mirror," the sequence of expanding symbols used by Guillaume and Jean can be seen to have for its purpose the enlightenment of the reader, who will most assuredly be tempted by the ways of the world. Guillaume's fountain is situated beneath a pine tree, the largest tree in the garden. The Lover, we are told, comes "To rest him in the shadowyng" of the fountain, which is "Springyng in a marble-stone" and bears the inscription "Here starfe the fayre Narcisus." He thereupon decides to drink from the fountain. Here is Chaucer's translation of the scene:

> And in the water anon was sene
> His nose, his mouthe, his eyen shene,
> And he thereof was al abasshed:
> His owne shadowe had him betrasshed.
> . . . . . . . . . . . . . . . . . . . . . . . . . . . . . .
> He lost his wytee right in that place,
> And deyde within a lytell space.
>
> (1517–36)

In a passage from the fountain scene, a passage that has puzzled some commentators on the poem, women are addressed as follows:

> Ladyes, I praye ensample taketh,
> Ye that ayenst your loue mistaketh;
> For if her dethe be you to wyte,
> God can ful wel your whyle quyte.
>
> (1539–42)

Some have asked why the ladies are addressed, but if the *Roman* parallels the biblical Fall, then most questions about this scene should be answered. Women were early blamed for Adam's (and man's) fall from grace. Whether the cause lay in Eve's curiosity, vanity, gullibility, or self-pride, it was her sensualism that traditionally undermined Adam's reason. This pattern is followed by Guillaume and Jean, and it is repeated in Milton's writings centuries later.

The use of this theme is, I believe, one reason for the fountain scene in *Paradise Lost*, and in more than one passage Eve's physical attractiveness is noted. Even Adam doubts whether he can withstand "the charm of Beauty's powerful glance." Raphael warns Adam of the difference between passion and love and relates in detail how Adam is the Head and Eve the Body (8.530–94). And in another illuminating passage Adam tells Raphael that "Love thou say'st / Leads up to Heav'n, is both the way and guide." This comment about love as the way and guide to heaven recalls other instances where guides are mentioned, and each of these passages reinforces a central theme of *Paradise Lost* and the *Roman:* the love of men and the love of God. When Eve, for example, is led astray by the "wat'ry shape," a "voice" warns her, and she is "invisibly thus *led*" to Adam, whom she rejects in favor of "that smooth wat'ry image."

In the opening lines of Book 5, when Eve relates her dream to Adam, the word *guide* is again used. This time, however, the guide is Satan. Something has changed since Eve's self-infatuation. Concerning her dream, Eve says that "a gentle voice," which she thought was Adam's, called her forth. Again, here is that confusion, and it is always the same: should she follow Adam, Satan, or God, and does she know the difference or the consequence of a choice? When the dream is shattered, this pattern receives additional emphasis when Eve remarks, "My Guide was gone." Still later in the poem, when Adam's creation is recounted, a dream stands at his head, "of shape Divine," which comes as a "guide" to lead him to the garden of bliss (8.292–99). But at the temptation scene in Book 9, Satan, having inhabited a serpent, guides Eve to the Forbidden Tree: "Lead then, said Eve. Hee leading swiftly roll'd / In tangles, and made intricate seem straight" (9.631–32). With her seduction underway and her fall imminent, it only remains for Adam to fall. Milton again highlights this central theme of love by turning Eve's seduction of Adam into a "glorious trial of exceeding Love." Adam subsequently places love of woman above love of God, and they burn in lust. This resultant action adds to an already established image pattern and enables the reader to watch Eve make a series of successively wrong choices concerning the proper kind of love. It is exactly this image pattern, exactly this technique, and exactly this dénouement that Guillaume and Jean utilize in the *Roman*.

As has been noted, it is the Lady who receives the blame for man's fall from grace and reason; this perhaps explains the misogyny frequently cited in the *Roman* and in *Paradise Lost*. Nevertheless, to return to the Fountain of Narcissus, the emphasis, as I remarked about a similar passage in Milton's poem, is on deception, on mistaken ideas about love, and on the overthrow of reason. Consider the two fountains in the *Roman*. In Guillaume's fount of Narcissus:

> Downe at the botome set sawe I
> Two cristall stones craftely

In Thilke fresshe and fayre well
. . . . . . . . . . . . . . . . . . . . . . .
For whan the sonne, clere in syght,
Cast in that welle his bemes bright,
And that the heete discended is,
Than taketh the cristall stone, ywis,
Agayne the sonne an hundred hewes,
. . . . . . . . . . . . . . . . . . . . . . . . . . . . . .
And all the yerde in it was sene.
. . . . . . . . . . . . . . . . . . . . . . . . .
For euer, in whiche halfe that [he] be,
[He] may halfe the gardyne se.

(1567–95)

Described as "the mirror perillus" and "the Wells of Loue," the Fountain of Narcissus has "now intriked" the Lover, who "in the snare . . . fell anone, / That had betrasshed many a one." Among the thousand things reflected in the mirror, he sees "A roser charged ful of rosis," and from it he chooses one bud. At this moment the God of Love lets fly an arrow "That Through myn eye vnto myn herte / The takel smote." Four arrows follow, and each one takes that path made so familiar by the literature of courtly love—through the eye to the heart. To note the holding power and endurance of this device, one has only to recognize its echoes even in *Paradise Lost* in those passages already discussed. The Lover then accepts the God of Love as his counsel, his confidant, and his liege lord. He thereby steels himself against the advice of reason, his conscience, and his rightful Lord. In language once again made familiar by Renaissance literature, he says to the God of Love:

And if ye lyst of me to make
Your prisoner, I wol it take
Of herte and wyll, fully at gre.
Holy and playne I yelde me,

> Without feynyng or heyntsye,
> To be gouerned by your emprise.

(1967–72)

This, then, is the same pattern Milton follows in detailing his story of the Fall. He is far more complex, weighty, and sublime than the French poets, but Milton had the weight of the Renaissance tradition behind, not before, him, and he was writing an epic, nor an epic romance. The pattern is, however, identical: Man looks into a glass darkly, and he sees himself darkly. The world is spread before him, and he foolishly chooses that transitory world with its fading love instead of that heavenly one with its unfading, celestial roses. When he makes this choice, he doffs his crown of reason and falls prey to his lower senses, represented by the God of Love or by the Devil—it makes little difference. If this story of a fall from grace seems like a twice-told tale, it is that, but in these particular instances it is much more. For these poems are much like Alanus's threefold mirror, which reflects, in turn, the Scriptures, Nature, and Man; and when one lays the books aside, perhaps he sees himself a little more clearly, a little less darkly.

Just as Milton juxtaposes images for the reader's benefit, so too does Jean de Meun. Thousands of lines after Guillaume's Fountain of Narcissus, Jean introduces its counterpart, the Well of the Trinity. It is found, not in a garden of delight, but in the Park of the Good Shepherd. Jean's fountain, of course, supersedes and surpasses Jean's fountain. It is not, Jean writes, the fountain that the Lover saw earlier because that one "makes well people ill!" But the fountain in the Park of the Good Shepherd

> Flows from a Triple Well, unfailing clear.
> These forces are so close together set
> That altogether gather in one stream
> So that when one sees all he can perceive

But one, or three in one—a Trinity.

. . . . . . . . . . . . . . . . . . . . . . . . . . . . .

For 'tis itself the source from which it flows;

. . . . . . . . . . . . . . . . . . . . . . . . . . . . . . . . . . .

'Tis its own conduit. . . .

(94. 143–56)


Furthermore, an olive tree, not a pine, shades Jean's fountain, and it "bears salvation's fruit." Reflected within its waters is a carbuncle:

> More marvelous than any precious stone,
> A round carbuncle, in three facets cut;
> So high it hangs that it lights all the park,
>
> . . . . . . . . . . . . . . . . . . . . . . . . . . . . . . . . .
>
> No sun illumines it, and yet it has
> So fine a color, and it shines so clear,
> That the resplendent sun which falls upon
> The double crystal in that other spring
> Would seem obscure and dull compared to it.
>
> (94. 189–207)


Anyone who looks into this fountain sees himself and all things contained within the park for what they are. Furthermore, "He who has seen/ Himself reflected there at once becomes/ So wise a master that he nevermore/ Can be deceived by ought that may occur" (94. 226–29).

On one level at least it is an easy choice, for Guillaume's fountain is a well of death and Jean's is a well of eternal life. The Lover is deceived when he gazes into the Well of Narcissus; those reflecting crystals are his own eyes. In effect, he falls in love with himself, with his own mortality, and thereby insures his own death. Those who look into Jean's Triple Well, illuminated by the carbuncle, see not the transience of man but the immortality of the wellspring of all life. If a man can relegate fast-fading flowers of the flesh to their proper place (as instruments to an end), then he can assure himself of immortality and the love of God. The Lover, like Eve, cannot do this; and, like the Lover, Eve, who is self-enthralled with her own beauty, eats the barren apple of mortality. This is probably represented by the inedible fruit of the pine tree, which shades the Lover and the Well of Narcissus. The fountain of life in Jean's garden, however, is shaded by an olive tree, whose powerfully symbolic fruit represents Christ and his selfless love for mankind. It is probably wise to note in passing that it could refer to the biblical prophecy that Christ will be born out of a root of Jesse (Isa. 11: 1). The people of the Middle Ages loved analogies, and because Mary was of the house of David (root of Jesse), Christ was the fruit of that royal line. If Eve was despoiled and spoiled by eating of the fruit, then Mary, the second Eve, was glorified and glorious in presenting the world with the fruit of the tree of Jesse. This imagery is used successfully by Jean and by Milton, and both works refer constantly to the shade or shadows of the well. As Robertson notes, the shade of the tree where Adam and Eve sought refuge is usually associated with *scientia*, or wordly wisdom conducive to a false sense of security ("Doctrine of Charity," p. 26). Much as the Lover is misled by his image in the well to become easy prey for the God of Love, who can easily represent the Devil or at least man's baser senses, so also is Eve misled by her own image, surely a sign of her future fall.

Eve is also misguided and misled by the Serpent-Tempter who is described as having carbuncle eyes (9. 500), an interesting parallel to the use of carbuncle in the *Roman*, whether it is understood in its lapidary sense of the stone found in the river of paradise or its meaning of "burning coal" or "lantern." The latter meaning closely resembles that time-honored image used by Courtly Love poets of "eyes darting contagious fire."[12] It may be noted in passing that the Serpent-Tempter is described as having carbuncle eyes only during his obsequious flattering of Eve. If we remember Robertson's belief that medieval artists symbolically replaced the serpent by Venus or Cupid,[13] an analogy can be made between the seduction of Eve by a serpent with carbuncle eyes and, in Guillaume's section of the *Roman,* the arrows of the God of Love entering the Lover's eyes and finding their way to his heart. Jean, in his section of the *Roman,* also uses the carbuncle for similar ends. As we have noted, the Triple Well in the Park of the Good Shepherd reflects not two crystals but, like the Fountain of Narcissus,

> A round carbuncle, in three facets cut:
> So high it hangs that it lights all the park,
> And one can see it plainly far away.
> . . . . . . . . . . . . . . . . . . . . . . . . . . . . . .
> No other sun
> But this carbuncle ever needs to shine.
> It is this garden's sun—its glow more bright
> Than any other that e'er shone on earth.
> . . . . . . . . . . . . . . . . . . . . . . . . . . . . . .
> It has a force
> So marvelous that whatsoever man
> Beholds it hanging there and then perceives
> His face reflected in the spring below
> Always from whatsoever side he looks,
> Sees all things contained within the park
> And recognizes each for what it is,
> And ever knows its worth. He who has seen
> Himself reflected there at once becomes
> So wise a master that he nevermore
> Can be deceived by aught that may occur.
> (94. 190–299)

Furthermore, the rays of this carbuncle

> never harm
> Or daze the eyes of those who on it gaze,

Or make them dizzy; it invigorates
Their eyesight and delights and strengthens it
By its clear beauty and its temperate heat.

(94. 231–36)

This passage is meant to nullify the obvious beauties of the
Garden of Deduit, or the ways of the flesh, and to turn the
reader toward the beauties of the Trinity, represented in
Jean's garden by the carbuncle. We should notice the parallels
with *Paradise Lost*. Whereas the reflecting crystals in the
Fountain of Narcissus (i.e., the Lover's own eyes) permit the
entry of the power of earthly beauty (i.e., the Rose and the
arrows of the God of Love into the Lover's heart), they become an end in themselves and stun the Lover, causing him to
lie down in the shadow of the pine and to lose his reason. The
reflection of the carbuncle in the Triple Well, however, does
just the opposite: it "invigorates the eyesight," and enables
those who see their reflection in this well to see reality, not
the falseness and transience of mundane life. Milton, I believe, lays this identical pattern before the eyes of the reader.
Of course, it is Eve who must undergo this literary trial, but
she remains oblivious of its meaning until after the Fall. Although she is given every opportunity to look into the mirror
of self, she deceives herself and falls.

Just as Jean may use the carbuncle to recall both its meanings (the stone found in the river of paradise and burning coal
or lantern), so too does Milton. We have already noted the
reflection made by the carbuncle in the Triple Well of the
Park of the Good Shepherd. This is its primary use. Jean,
however, concludes this section concerning the Park of the
Good Shepherd when Genius

amidst the throng
. . . threw the waxen torch, whose smoking flame
Sets fire to all the world. No woman lives
Who can resist it. Venus spreads the fire

. . . . . . . . . . . . . . . . . . . . . . . . . . . . . . . . .
News of the charter then did Cupid spread
Until all valiant men were quite agreed thereto.
                                        (94.297–305)

Moments afterward (following the Pygmalion interpolation),
Venus sets the Tower of the Rose aflame. These actions are
undoubtedly related to the earlier actions in Guillaume's Garden of Deduit when the God of Love inflames the Lover with
the beauty of the Rose. Just as this leads to the Lover's self-
enthrallment in Guillaume's part of the *Roman*, it leads in
Jean's continuation to the attack on the Castle of the Rose
and to her dénouement, which is incited by Venus who lets
fly "Her feathered arrow full of flaming fire," setting fire to
the castle. Milton specifically mentions carbuncle only in
Book 9 at the temptation scene, and its use, I think, shows
correspondence not only with its meaning of "burning coal"
or "lantern" but also to the image of concupiscence as used by
Jean de Meun. The passage certainly bears overtones of the
language of Courtly Love and of seduction:

> So spake the Enemy of Mankind, enclos'd
> In Serpent, Inmate bad, and toward Eve
> Address'd his way, not with indented wave,
> Prone on the ground, as since, but on his rear,
> Circular base of rising folds, that tow'r'd
> Fold above fold a surging Maze, his Head
> Crested aloft, and Carbuncle his Eyes;
> With burnisht Neck of verdant Gold, erect
> Amidst his circling Spires, that on the grass
> Floated redundant: pleasing was his shape,
> And lovely.
>                                        (9.494–504)

Whether the Serpent-Tempter seduces Eve sexually is a moot
point; however, the figurative apparatus is definitely here,

and the same pattern is repeated: Eve is beguiled, Eve refuses to listen to reason, Eve falls. We have watched the same chain of events before—when she becomes enamored of her own reflection and when she is inspired by Satan during her dream. Moreover, many of the same words are repeated from these earlier passages. Water imagery is emphasized: "indented wave," "surging Maze," "floated redundant," and (from the same scene, nine lines later) "As when a Ship by Skilful Steersman wrought / Nigh River's mouth or Foreland, Where the Wind / Veers oft, as oft so steers, and shifts her Sail; / So varied hee."

In addition, the passage includes the Protean image of disguise, seen in the references to water, in the fact that Satan has assumed the form of a serpent, in the insistence upon his "pleasing shape, / And lovely," and at the unexpected allusion to Circe and "the Herd disguis'd" (9.522). An equally heavy stress is placed on the visual aspects of the scene: the Serpent has "Carbuncle Eyes"; he "Curl'd many a wanton wreath in sight of *Eve*, / To lure her Eye (9.517–18); he stands "as in gaze admiring" (9.524); and his expression "turn'd at length / The Eye of Eve to mark his play" (9.527–28). In this passage, then, I believe that Milton reinforces and iterates his central theme of mistaken love by interrelating it figuratively and imaginatively to preceding passages. In addition, just as the *Roman* incorporates images of both fire and water in the fountains and in the heat of lust (and in the use of carbuncle), Milton also uses this technique in *Paradise Lost*. As the Lover becomes self-enthralled at the fountain and burns in lust at the Castle of the Rose, so also does Eve. She becomes enamored of herself, like the Lover, at the reflecting stream, and she and Adam burn in lust after the Fall.

But there are additional ramifications. If we accept Venus and the God of Love as symbolic replacements for Satan, we must not forget that Venus was born out of the sea from the severed genitalia of Saturn. Water therefore becomes a sym-

bol of Venus, of lust.[14] One of the meanings that we have
seen ascribed to the carbuncle is "stone from the river of
paradise." If this description is appropriate to Venus and
Saturn, it is even more appropriate to Satan, who was certainly created in the very river or mirror of paradise—the
Godhead Itself. Even his name "Lucifer" is akin to another
accepted meaning of carbuncle, "burning coal" or "lantern."
Furthermore, we must not neglect in any appraisal of these
passages in the *Roman* and in *Paradise Lost* the references to
the Virgin. If water is variously used to suggest Venus, Satan,
lust, *speculum*, self-knowledge, the Trinity, Christ, error and
self-delusion, we must also mention the Virgin, who has been
symbolized in iconography and literature by both a mirror
and a well.[15] Because Mary, according to allegorical interpretation of the Song of Songs, was a mirror or a well of waters
or a fountain sealed, she produced the "image" or "thought"
of God (the *Imago*). This was, of course, Christ, who
through Mary was made visible to the eyes of the flesh.[16] Eve,
in *Paradise Lost*, is vividly connected with water imagery,
which has just been discussed. The Rose in the *Roman* also is
closely related with water imagery. And each of these two
characters, I believe, iconographically and allegorically represents the Virgin Mary. We must also remember that both Eve
and the Rose initially are virgins, a point important to both
poems. Both of them, however, are depicted to resemble
Venus and to evoke the train of associations invariably associated with that goddess. One can also cite here the allegorical dichotomy of the "twin Venuses," which Spenser, among
many others, uses so successfully in *The Faerie Queene*. But
Eve and the Rose—and by extension the Lover—totally neglect the mirror within themselves (the Imago) and become
instead beguiled by the reflection of the temporal world,
which is represented by their own reflection or shadow (imago). The Virgin Mary, however, whose vision was forever
clear and unblurred, looked into the mirror of self and saw

reflected in it, not the transient world of man, but the *Imago* which was Christ and immortality. Hers was a totally selfless love, and she was spared the flame of lust.

Those who feel that such a juxtaposition of Eve with Mary in *Paradise Lost* or of the Rose with Mary in the *Roman* is strained must be reminded that Milton several times in *Paradise Lost* makes the comparison between Eve and Mary, at one point even referring to Mary as the second Eve. But the comparison was a commonplace in the Middle Ages, and, as Albert C. Labriola implies, the *Canticum Canticorum* gave an early precedent for considering divine love in terms of cupidinous love; furthermore, he states that the Canticles may be used as a frame of reference to interpret *Paradise Lost*.[17] I agree and certainly believe that it would be worthwhile to use the Song of Songs as a gloss on the *Roman*.[18] Thomas Kranidas, in discussing Adam and Eve in the garden, perhaps summarizes this juxtaposition of sacred and profane best as "Sensuality and the annunciation, the paradox of the *felix culpa* within the comedy of fruits of trees and wombs and the potential implication of angels and readers in the nakedness of Eve."[19] Although the comic aspects are far more readily apparent in the *Roman* than they are in *Paradise Lost*, they are present in the latter work, and they point to still another correspondence between these two great works.

Of course, other images and patterns reinforce one another in the authors under discussion. Jean's well, for example, must be analyzed very carefully. While it purports to be a "true" fountain in a "true" garden, and in many ways it should be read as such, the reader must never forget the impassioned paean to unbridled fecundity as the means of man's salvation, lyrical praise given moments before the description of the Park of the Good Shepherd (11.19,505–19,906, chap. 91 in Robbins). Nor must the reader forget the account of Jupiter's reign and his castration, which also precedes the section on the good garden. Nor must one forget that Genius concludes the sermon on the Park by throwing the waxen torch, an act that leads to the final assault on the Castle of the Rose. These passages are certainly antithetical to the message of the sermon on the Park of the Good Shepherd, which they enclose.

When it is understood, however, that the *Roman* and *Paradise Lost* treat almost exclusively the problem of sin and sinning, that both works see that problem as a necessary corollary of the sin of Adam and Eve, and that they use the seduction of man as a vehicle to present a well-known story, these similarities are, of necessity, more interesting. And it is particularly informative to note how Milton and Guillaume and Jean lead not only their characters but also their readers to an identical fountain. Moreover, the authors, through the beauties of character, setting, and verse, encourage their readers to drink deeply, thereby permitting them to ensnare themselves. So when critics speak wryly of Eve's obvious voluptuousness; of the literary technique of letting the reader furtively gaze at Adam and Eve in their bower, all the while realizing that he sees the couple through Satan's lecherous stare; of Milton's "Satanic style";[20] of the sensual description of the garden itself, they must begin to realize that Milton was fully aware of this evocative power. Spenser uses an identical technique in *The Faerie Queene* (Bk.2.12, the "Bower of Bliss" sections), which at times nearly causes the reader to feel like a voyeur. But Milton and Spenser had a well-known example of literary "naughtiness" always before them. Surely, it becomes more and more evident that the ribald nature of the *Roman* is little more than a well-baited hook to snare the unwary reader. Is this not exactly the reason and purpose for the interpolated tale of Vulcan's discovery of Venus and Mars caught in the nets of love? (63.1–265; or 11.13,847–14,186 in the original French MS). Is this not another rhetorical device that repeats and reinforces the central message of the *Roman*—and *Paradise Lost:* that man unwarily enthralls himself in the false beauties of the flesh? But, to return to the fountain scenes themselves, one must note their similarity of structure and purpose.

Both fountain scenes occur early in their respective tales, and both become central to later developments in the poems. The Lover, although he has been given entrance into the garden by *Luxuria* and has joined with others in the Old Dance, does walk away from the sportive couples. The occasion of *sinning* has been presented to him, but it is only at the well, however, that he accepts the invitation to sensual love, that he doffs his crown of reason, and that he allegorically becomes liege man to the God of Love. Similarly, the newly created Eve, wandering aimlessly in a similar garden setting, is almost immediately tested at a well. Only a heavenly voice and the restraint of Adam, who "with [his] gentle hand / Seiz'd [hers]" (4.488–89), prevent Eve from returning to her image. Eve, like her counterpart in the *Roman*, is a "wandring Soule," which, as Labriola points out, is an emblem used by Quarles to refer to those who leave the sanctified relationship with the Godhead and become an "hourly prey" of sins.[21] Eve and the Lover become the prey of the God of Love and of Satan, the one following and shooting arrows, the other disguising himself and seeking her out.

No matter what explanation is given for these episodes at the well (and there are many), it is never for Eve's or the Lover's benefit, but for the reader's; for, as Fish points out in *Paradise Lost*, Eve (and the Lover) remain oblivious of its import. As I have noted earlier, much of the imagery of Eve's reflection scene is repeated at the scene when Satan inspires Eve's dreaming. Moreover, at the fatal seduction scene, more of this imagery reappears. Satan is, of course, disguised or self-inbruted, a point noted earlier for its Protean and iconographic associations. Self-fallen himself, Satan yearns to debase others in order to fit them to that hell he knows so well. As Satan approaches Eve, Milton's verse is characterized by water imagery, which I have noted is suggestive of the fountain. Just as the Lover sins first by looking at and loving his own reflection in the water, then by idolizing the Rosebud, and finally be being stricken in the eyes by the arrows of the God of Love, so too is this pattern repeated in relation to Eve. First she sees her own image and prefers it to Adam; then she becomes easier prey as Satan inspires her dreams; and then she marks the serpent's "play" with wonder. The Serpent's shape, we have noted, "pleasing was . . . / And lovely" as he gazed insatiate at Eve. His words make their way "Into the Heart of Eve." And Milton repeats: "his words replete with guile / Into her heart too easy entrance won" (9.733–34). It is also interesting that Satan finds Eve, his destined prey, in a "Spring of Roses" (9.218) and that the interdicted apple tree is "Fast by a Fountain" (9.628).

It should now be apparent that the images, scenes, and themes within the garden settings of the *Roman de la Rose* and *Paradise Lost* are parallel. As I have shown, similarities between the late-seventeenth-century work and the thirteenth-century work abound. Both authors, it is true, work out of and within an ancient tradition. Concerning the Middle Ages, Robertson notes, "Profane letters were thought of as being allegorical in much the same way as the Bible is allegorical."[22] It would be naive to assume that Milton overlooked the didactic purpose and intentions of the *Roman*. Because the *Roman* seems (on one level) to be about the adulterous relationship between the Lover and the Rose, this concern does not preclude its seriousness as a work of art. Robertson, citing John the Scot, says that *woman* represents the sensible beauty of all creatures and that *adultery* is a figure for all the vices or for a cupidinous desire (*Preface to Chaucer*, p. 71). "All error," Robertson continues, "thus begins in the exterior or aesthetic region of the garden, and through its delight in the phantasy of a beauty which it falsifies, it may corrupt and pervert the inner region of the garden, just as Eve successfully tempted Adam in the Fall" (ibid.). It should be sufficiently clear that the fountain scenes in the *Roman* and *Paradise Lost* are symbolic both of the Fall and of man's continual fall, and that both works seek to effect a change in man's nature, which has been perverted since that original Fall. The nearly parallel fountain scenes (Guillaume's, Jean's, and Milton's) are striking. The fountain, the tree, the shade and shadows, the shapes, the roses, and the reflection compose a tableau, and, in effect, they are one. And the symbolic value of all of these images can be found in various emblem books, for example, Quarles's or Hawkins's. The Lover's selection of a *budding* rose, for example, can be representative of the Second Coming: Christ is the Fruit of Mary, who is herself of the House of David, of which Jesse is the root.

But we must never forget, as some critics have, that Guillaume's *and* Milton's gardens have suggestions or overtones of evil or of fallen nature. Much, certainly, has been implied about the sensuous luxuriance of Milton's Garden of Eden.[23] However, we must remember that externals are never evil in themselves; Eve's beauty, for example, is not flawed or inherently evil; neither, for that matter, is the beauty of the Rose, the Garden of Deduit, its frolicking lovers, nor the Fountain of Narcissus. The perversion, as Robertson notes, occurs in the libido, the cupidity. Only when the senses internalize the object can it become dangerous: "If the thought pleasurably contemplates cupidinous satisfaction, the result is evil: The downfall of the reason and the corruption of the garden are disinct possibilities. On the other hand, if the thought refers the beauty of the image to the creator, all is well. The man retains his hierarchical ascendancy over the 'woman'; the spirit continues to guide its servant the body; the beauty of the *woman* remains innocent" *(Preface to Chaucer,* p. 72).

Here, then, are the reasons for the insistence by each author upon shadow and shape and seeing and hearing. The role carried out by the Serpent-Tempter is analogous to that of the God of Love: both represent illicit or cupidinous desire, and both lead their respective "mirror-gazers" into the cesspool of mortality. Both reject the guide who would lead them to a contemplation of God and eternity (Adam in *Paradise Lost* and Reason in the *Roman*, who both also function in nearly identical ways); both turn, instead, to the guide who will lead them down the path of dalliance and destruction. But, as I have earlier pointed out, these falls are foregone conclusions because everyone knows the fate of Adam and Eve, and everyone also knows that the Lover will pluck his Rose. These expectations aside, it is the reader whose fate lies in the balance. Just as the external beauties of the gardens and its characters are not evil, neither are the poems evil; they are beautiful works whose aims are to re-create Nature. If a reader is swayed by the beauties of Milton's verse or by his depiction of Eve's physical perfections, he may also be reminded of his fallen nature. If a reader is shocked by Guillaume's or Jean's story, or by Reason's use of "dirty words," he has fallen into the same snare that foiled the Lover and Adam and Eve. But if a reader *understands* the words, if he is able to juxtapose similar scenes and images in the *Roman* and *Paradise Lost* with similar occurrences in Scripture or in his own life, if he internalizes these images and uses them to contemplate his creator, then he can be saved. If, however, he fails to do this, then the *Roman* is an old lascivious tale and *Paradise Lost* becomes little more than an overly long exercise in reading. You pay your money and you take your choice, as the old saying goes. But the identical choice must be made for both works; for Milton was still embroidering the same fabric, begun in the days of Guillaume de Lorris, added to by Jean de Meun and hundreds of others, and perhaps completed by John Milton. The resultant piece of work is glorious and complete: the literary enclosed garden.[24]

# Notes

1. Sister Ritamary Bradley, "Backgrounds of the Title *Speculum* in Mediaeval Literature," *Speculum* 29 (1954):112. Sister Bradley cites the *Summa de Arte Predictoria* of Alanus de Insulis from the *Patrologia Latina*, ed. J. P. Migne (Paris, 1855), vol. 210, 118.

2. Many scholars have commented upon the influence of the *Roman* upon *Paradise Lost*. Among them are the following: A Bartlett Giamatti, *The Earthly Paradise and the Renaissance Epic* (Princeton, N.J.: Princeton University Press, 1966); John V. Fleming, *The Roman de la Rose: A Study in Allegory and Iconography* (Princeton, N.J.: Princeton University Press, 1969); and Albert C. Labriola, "The Aesthetics of Self-Diminution: Christian Iconography and *Paradise Lost*, In *"Eyes Fast Fixt": Current Perspectives in Milton Methodology, Milton Studies* 7, ed. Albert C. Labriola and Michael Lieb (Pittsburgh, Pa.: University of Pittsburgh Press, 1975). Of these, only Labriola's article cites specific similarities. Howard R. Patch in *The Goddess Fortuna in Medieval Literature* (Cambridge, Mass.: Harvard University Press, 1957); and Joseph E. Duncan in *Milton's Earthly Paradise: A Historical Study of Eden*, Minnesota Monographs in the Humanities 5 (Minneapolis: University of Minnesota Press, 1969) both warn about forcing correspondence between the two works.

3. John Milton, "The Commonplace Book," *The Works of John Milton*, ed. Frank Allen Patterson, et al. (New York: Columbia University Press, 1931–42), 18:195.

4. James Holly Hanford, "The Chronology of Milton's Private Studies," *Publications of the Modern Language Association* 36 (1921): 276, n. 113.

5. In *Th' Upright Heart and Pure*, ed. Father Amadeus P. Fiore (Pittsburgh, Pa.: Duquesne University Press, 1967), p. 80.

6. "Free Love and Free Will in *Paradise Lost*," *Studies in English Literature* 7 (1967): 95.

7. In this discussion I rely on the following editions: *The Romaunt of the Rose and Le roman de la Rose: A Parallel-Text Edition*, ed. Ronald Sutherland (Berkeley and Los Angeles: University of California Press, 1968). Since what is usually called Chaucer's translation is incomplete, references to the last portion of the *Roman* will be taken from *The Romance of the Rose*, trans. Harry Wolcott Robbins, ed. Charles W. Dunn (New York: E. P. Dutton, 1962). All references from these editions will be given parenthetically. The first number in references to the Robbins translation refers to the chapters into which he has divided the *Roman*.

8. All references from *Paradise Lost* are from *John Milton: Complete Poems and Major Prose*, ed. Merritt Y. Hughes (New York: Odyssey Press, 1957). All subsequent references will be given parenthetically.

9. Although allegorical interpretation—its history, theory, and practice—is obviously a vast, unsettled issue, these studies provide various contemporary views. Among others that could be cited, see especially the following: Edward A. Bloom, "The Allegorical Principle," *English Literary History* 18 (1951): 163–90; Edwin Honig, *Dark Conceit: The Making of Allegory* (Evanston, Ill.: Northwestern University Press, 1959); Angus Fletcher, *Allegory: The Theory of a Symbolic Mode* (Ithaca, N.Y.: Cornell University Press, 1964); Michael Murrin, *The Veil of Allegory* (Chicago: University of Chicago Press, 1969); John MacQueen, *Allegory* (London: Methuen, 1970); and John M. Steadman, *The Lamb and the Elephant: Ideal*

*Imitation and the context of Renaissance Allegory* (San Marino, Calif.: The Huntington Library, 1974).

Also see Foster Provost's illuminating essay, which mentions the above works, "Treatments of Theme and Allegory in Twentieth-Century Criticism of *The Faerie Queene*" in *Contemporary Thought on Edmund Spenser*, ed. Richard C. Frushell and Bernard J. Vondersmith (Carbondale and Edwardsville: Southern Illinois University Press, 1975).

10. See especially Stanley Fish, *Surprised by Sin: The Reader in "Paradise Lost"* (New York: Macmillan, 1967) and the same author's article, "Discovery as Form in *Paradise Lost*," in *New Essays on Paradise Lost* ed. Thomas Kranidas (Berkeley: University of California Press, 1969), pp. 1–14.

11. Milton, a prophet in an age considerably dimmed by changing values, tastes, and styles, apparently turned first to drama as a vehicle for his major opus, and rejected it. He also turned from the romances, which he nevertheless read and admired. The *Arthuriad*, for which he had made sketchy plans, would probably have been developed on lines of the epic romance. Finally, he set his hand to writing an epic, *Paradise Lost*.

12. For a discussion of the meanings ascribed to gems and stones, see John Evans and Mary S. Serjeantson, *English Mediaeval Lapidaries*, no. 190, Early English Text Society (London: Oxford University Press, 1933).

13. D. W. Robertson, Jr., *A Preface to Chaucer: Studies in Medieval Perspectives* (Princeton, N.J.: Princeton University Press, 1962), p. 388.

14. George Boas, *Essays on Primitivism and Related Ideas in the Middle Ages* (1948; reprint ed. New York: Octagon Books, 1966), p. 159.

15. For example, see Henry Hawkins, *Parthenia Sacra* (1633), in D. M. Rogers, *English Recusant Literature* (Yorkshire, Scolar Press, 1971), 81:210–30.

16. Frederick Goldin, *The Mirror of Narcissus in the Courtly Love Lyric* (Ithaca, N.Y.: Cornell University Press, 1967), p. 4.

17. Albert C. Labriola, "The Aesthetics of Self-Diminution": Christian Iconography and *Paradise Lost*," in *"Eyes Fast Fixt": Current Perspectives in Milton Methodology*, *Milton Studies*, ed. Albert C. Labriola and Michael Lieb (Pittsburgh, Pa.: University of Pittsburgh Press, 1975), 7:283.

18. Although this study cannot begin to explore the relevance of the *Canticum Canticorum* to the *Roman* or to *Paradise Lost*, I believe that such a study could only give additional support to the thesis of this discussion. Note, for example, *The Targum to the Song of Songs*, trans. from Aramaic by Herman Gollancz (London: Luzac and Co., 1909), p. 21, where the targum (paraphrase) to the line, "As the rose among thorns, so is my love among the daughters," is given as follows: "But when I turn aside from the path straight before me, and He removeth his Holy Presence from me, I am likened to the rose that blossometh forth among the thorns, which pierce and tear the branches, in the same manner as I am pierced and torn by the evil decrees (endured) in exile at the hands of the kings of the nations." One can certainly find parallels between this and the *Roman* and *Paradise Lost*. In addition, see Robert Gordis, *The Song of Songs: A Study, Modern Translation and Commentary*, vol. 20, Texts and Studies of the Jewish Theological Seminary of America (1954), who states that the first allegorical treatment of the Song of Songs was written in the early third century by Hippolytus of Rome (p. 3). He further states that "the only justifiable conclusion is that the *Song of Songs*, like the Psalter, is an anthology, running a wide gamut of its emotions. It contains songs of love's yearning and its consummation, of coquetry and passion, of separation and union, of courtship and marriage" (pp. 17–

18). This quotation by Gordis could certainly be used as a thematic summary of the *Roman*, if not of *Paradise Lost*.

19. "Adam and Eve in the Garden: A Study of *Paradise Lost*, book V," *Studies in English Literature*, 4 (1964): p. 78.

20. See A. Bartlett Giamatti's chapter on the garden in *Paradise Lost* in *The Earthy Paradise and the Renaissance Epic* (Princeton, N.J.: Princeton University Press, 1966), pp. 299 ff.

21. Labriola, "Aesthetics of Self-Diminution," p. 287. See also Quarles's *Emblemes* (London, 1635), p. 237.

22. "The Doctrine of Charity in Mediaeval Literary Gardens: A Topical Approach Through Symbolism and Allegory," *Speculum* 26 (1951): 25.

23. Perhaps Giamatti's discussion is the most helpful.

24. I am heavily indebted to ideas found in Stanley N. Stewart's discussion of the enclosed garden in his excellent book *The Enclosed Garden: The Tradition and the Image in Seventeenth-Century Poetry* (Madison: University of Wisconsin Press, 1966).

# Personalia

PAUL M. DOWLING is Associate Professor of English at Canisius College in Buffalo, New York. His dissertation at the University of Indiana dealt with Milton's prose style, and he is currently preparing a book on Milton's *Areopagitica*.

ELLEN GOODMAN is Assistant Professor of English at Providence College in Providence, Rhode Island. She has written on Walt Whitman as well as Milton, and is presently finishing a book on Milton entitled "The Design of Milton's World: Nature and the Fall in Christian Genesis Commentary and *Paradise Lost*."

ALBERT C. LABRIOLA is Professor of English at Duquesne University. His publications on Milton and Renaissance studies have appeared in many periodicals, including *Modern Language Studies, Milton Quarterly*, and the *Huntington Library Quarterly*. He was a major contributor to the *Milton Encyclopedia*, and he co-edited *Milton Studies* with Michael Lieb in 1975.

MICHAEL LIEB is Professor of English at the University of Illinois, Chicago Circle. He has published four books on Milton and numerous articles; the most recent have appeared in the *Harvard Theological Review* and *Studies in English Literature*.

WILLIAM MELCZER is Professor of Comparative Literature at Syracuse University. He has published numerous articles on Renaissance Humanism both here and abroad; his most recent book is *Les Dialoghi d'amore de Léon l'Hébreu*, published in the series Textes et documents de la Renaissance (Paris: Vrin, 1980).

JOHN MULRYAN is Professor of English at Saint Bonaventure University. He has published widely on Milton, Spenser, and other poets of the period, and is presently completing a book on Spenser and the mythological tradition.

PAUL F. REICHARDT teaches in the Department of Language and Literature at Drury College in Springfield, Missouri. He has frequently spoken at the Kalamazoo Medieval Conference, and is presently continuing his research on Milton's relationship to the iconographical tradition.

JASON P. ROSENBLATT is Associate Professor of English at Georgetown University. He has published on both Milton and Shakespeare, and his articles have appeared in *Publications of the Modern Language Association, English Literary History,* and the *Shakespeare Quarterly.* He studied the conflicting traditions in *Paradise Lost* as a Guggenheim Fellow in 1977 and 1978.

EDWARD SICHI JR., is assistant professor of English at the McKeesport campus of the Pennsylvania State University. He has published extensively on Milton, Faulkner, and the *Roman de la Rose* in *Cithara, Milton Studies,* and other periodicals.

JOHN C. ULREICH, JR. is Associate Professor of English at the University of Arizona. He has published articles on Milton in *Milton Studies,* the *Milton Quarterly,* and *Studies in English Literature.*

# Index